Praise for Different Drummers authors, Kevin Cummings and John Gartland

"Cummings writes in a warm and humble voice devoid of literary pretensions or highfalutin prose, reminding readers of one of Bangkok's chief virtues: it's teeming with all sorts of eccentric expat characters endowed with hugely entertaining backstories."

Jim Algie – author of *The Phantom Lover and Other Thrilling Tales of Thailand*

"*Different Drummers* is another fascinating ensemble of interviews, literature reviews, stories and poetry about Thailand and the region."

Melissa Ray – four time Muay Thai Champion in Thailand

"John Gartland's poetry brutally and beautifully exposes hypocrisy and despair, in a world of manipulated madness. Gartland is a master poet in the tradition of Seamus Heaney."

Christopher Minko – Front man for Cambodian band, Krom

"No other expat author in Thailand writes with such lyrical artistry."

The Nation of John Gartland

Different Drummers

KEVIN CUMMINGS

with poetry by

JOHN GARTLAND

This book is dedicated to the memory of
four important Different Drummers in my family:

PAPA JOHN CUNNINGHAM
AND HIS THREE CHILDREN.
ALISTAIR. ARCHIE. AND MARION

And to the most important beat of all,

RATREE

"The road to Hell is paved with works-in-progress."
—PHILIP ROTH

"Mmmm, Juicy Fruit."
—KEN KESEY

Mark Fenn was, among many other more important things, the Editor in Chief for my first book, *Bangkok Beat*. Mark died suddenly in the early morning hours at his home in Chiang Mai in 2016, and it is a loss that continues to shock.

Mark and I spoke a lot on the phone, and, with his British accent, he always sounded so polite. He would handle comments like that with a balance of professionalism, candor, humor, and, of course, politeness.

I sought Mark out for the job because I knew he had recently parted ways as Editor at Chiang Mai City News. I also knew there would be a lot of work involved, turning dozens of blog posts and a handful of new stories into a readable book. There was, and he never complained. He did the hard work, and turned the 75,000 words mess I gave him into a book I am proud of, and a book, as he told me many times, he enjoyed reading. Authors can go through periods of doubt and I was no different. Beyond our many phone calls there were hundreds of text messages regarding the editing of *Bangkok Beat*. Mark made it clear that he enjoyed the stories in *Bangkok Beat*. "It's the kind of book I like to read", he said. Then he would reassure me by adding, characteristically, "I'm not blowing smoke up your ass."

I finally met Mark face to face at the book launch for *Bangkok Beat* on July 26th, 2015. Mark and his wife, Ning, were so helpful and pleasant throughout the event. They had taken the overnight bus from

Chiang Mai to be there, and Mark was pleased to have booked a good hotel room along the Chao Praya River. Mark was a history buff, so it was no surprise he chose the River of Kings over a closer Sukhumvit Road location to spend time with Ning. He warned me that he had grown a mustache and that reactions were "mixed". There was no need to worry. I liked Mark Fenn, and I am still saddened at his early passing.

I used to joke with Mark that I didn't know how bad a writer I was until I got around good editors. I received editorial advice from many, but Mark did the heavy lifting.

One can learn a lot from writing a book. And the lessons are not all about writing. They are about the journey and the people you meet along the way. I am fortunate to have met and got to know Mark, briefly, during mine.

With, or without that moustache, Mark Fenn was a good and loyal man. I miss him.

INTRODUCTION

By Paul Dorsey

For my own safety I'd long ago been evacuated from the feverish nocturnal emissions of downtown Bangkok, leaving the scene entombed, I'm sure, in concrete despair at my departure. It had something to do with the asbestos lining in the walls of the bars, my then-wife told me. That seemed doubtful, because those bars BURNED. But she was usually wiser than me (and hence has since left).

In my cozy cocoon in the safer, greener suburbs, I was free to mull the memories while shielded from the frights. And then one day a grey slab landed on my desk bearing an intricate hieroglyphic etching by Colin Cotterill. It was the original "Bangkok Beat", forerunner of this book, and its author was soon sending me e-tom-toms summoning me to a gathering of the tribe far up the Sukhumvit River, deep in the heart of that very darkness I'd fled, at a landing called Check Inn 99.

I readily accepted because "Bangkok Beat" had been fun to read, a re-acquaintance with writers whose work I knew and an introduction to many I'd never heard of, plus the story of this ancient watering hole where Bob Hope had filmed "Road to Danang", co-starring Madame Noi, who still worked there (Check Inn, not Danang). And anyway, these were literary types and surely they wouldn't be hitting me up for phaeng maak lady drinks. Not immediately, anyway.

Kevin, of course, hadn't written about go-go bars, even if the noir authors and poets he profiled made them a trade staple, or at least they'd used all that red-light Bangkok sordidness as a backdrop for their gumshoe whodunnits and spook escapades. Kevin wrote about the joy of reading and of discovering new writers, about what made the local literary talents tick, and how they compared with the world's greats.

So, yeah, I had to meet the guy.

Offsetting my intense disappointment at not being introduced to Mama Noi on that first visit to Check Inn or a subsequent one, which were the only two times I got to see the apparently unsinkable cabaret at the actual location of its birth, were three things:

- Proprietor Chris Catto-Smith proved to be an immensely entertaining raconteur in his own right (and popped for my steak dinner);
- Kevin Cummings proved to be as interesting as any hanger-on could hope for, a Californian former skateboarder and hoop-slamming hero so well connected in the creative community in Thailand and Cambodia that I still haven't fully fathomed his Facebook feed.
- These guys, for all their early, hangover-free rising the next day and their dedication to the keyboard, proved to like drinking as much as I did.

"Bangkok Beat" did such a neat job of name-dropping that I was inspired to get on with an old ambition to make a list of all the expatriate writers who'd ever produced books about or set in Thailand. Done. It now has its own Facebook group.

In the past three years, I've had the pleasure to read and review fiction and non-fiction books by John Gartland, Collin Piprell, Jim Algie, Christopher G Moore, John Burdett, Matt Carrell and James Newman, all frequently mentioned names in the "Bangkok Beat" circle.

I've become acquainted with dozens more people in the circle and on the fringes, some not even writers, although I keep telling John Fengler, the most interesting of these folks, that he ought to be a writer. Through Kevin Cummings I also met Chris Coles, Eric Nelson, Gary Rutland, Christopher Minko, Mark Bolam, Alasdair McLeod, Ian Donnelly, Bruce Scott, Dean Barrett, a musical frog named Gop and some joker named Doug Stanhope. Countless more of his friends have become mine online.

Now I'm doing the name-dropping. It's good to get out of the cocoon once in a while.

In my newspaper review of "Bangkok Beat", I tagged Kevin as the "chronicler of the noir night", the local literary movement's historian, probing their dark tales with a flashlight, interviewing them for his *Thailand Footprint* blog and then deciding to emulate them and put out a book of his own. It got solid reviews from me and many others. At last, three years on, we have the follow-up. Based on the evidence I have seen, I'm betting it will have been well worth the wait.

– PAUL DORSEY,
October 2018 Journalist and Book Reviewer
for *The Nation* Newspaper

Contents

CHAPTER 1

The Entertainment Zones

Five bits of cultural advice for Patpong, Nana Plaza & Soi Cowboy. Lest anyone think I am ignoring the three well-known entertainment areas in Bangkok, in this personal journey, well, I am … kinda.

There are, after all, tons of books out there that deal with them, and not enough that deal with all the other interesting happenings that go on in Bangkok and beyond. My focus is on the latter, since this book has a broader interest to pursue.

But truth be told, these three areas can never be ignored, entirely. "Density and velocity", is how artist Chris Coles described the attraction of the Bangkok night. The reality is, of the 21 million + + visitors Bangkok gets ever year – a number growing by leaps and bounds – more go to these three zones than all the temples combined, despite what you may read from the Tourism Authority of Thailand. Bangkok, has now been recognized as the top travel destination in the world by Lonely Planet Travel Guides and Mastercard International.

So herewith, I present all the cultural advice you will ever need to know about Nana Plaza, Soi Cowboy and Patpong:

1. Never, ever go to an upstairs bar in Patpong even if you are, hypothetically, with a good mate that is Thai from your hometown in the USA.
2. If you do go to an upstairs bar in Patpong you will be ripped off, even if you are, hypothetically, with a good Thai mate that had lived in Bangkok for over twenty years.

3. By all means check out the culture of Nana Plaza. Everyone has. Mick Jagger has. Anthony Bourdain has. Husbands and wives have. Christian fundamentalists have. Groups of white women have. Groups of Arab men have tried. Go. Check it out. Be appalled. Be titillated. Don't be a jerk but be something and go.

4. Soi Cowboy: Walk up and down the small street. Be surprised how small the street is. Be amazed at what goes on in such a small street. Eat outside. Look at the people. Some will look back. It's not always easy to differentiate the animals from the spectators at this holy city zoo. Eat the street food. Eat an insect, just so you can say you did. The pyropes pesticide levels in one or two grasshoppers won't kill you. After that you are on your own.

5. Don't drink too much alcohol. It's poison to the body just like the pesticide in the insects. The body's response to them both is the same – let's get rid of this stuff before it does any more damage. Best to practice moderation in eating insects, and moderation in drinking alcohol. Take the middle path or the deep fried larvae. "Up to you" as the saying goes.

So there you have it. After you've been to all three entertainment areas, or as Meatloaf says, "Two out of three ain't bad", eaten your insects and been in the same places as Mick Jagger and company, congratulate yourself. You're in Bangkok, Thailand. And there are at least one-thousand other things you can see, eat, listen to, and do next. Better get started right after you read some of this book. Life is short. Bon Appetit!

CHAPTER 2

The Drum Beats of Technology

"We judge time by technology. We judge information by the date of the technology. Time is an exact messenger. I've decided to be a typewriter fundamentalist. I don't change with the times. You don't hear much about us, but of course you wouldn't. We're not online or in a chat room. But we know we are out there."

"You won't last. You'll be back on the computer before the day is over."
Crackdown, Chapter 25 by Christopher G. Moore

Recently I read two newspaper articles regarding technology that gave me pause. Of course they weren't actually read on paper; they were read online. I don't buy or read many actual newspapers nowadays. A sign of the technological times.

The articles are:
Why We Can't Look Away From Our Screens written in the *New York Times* on March 6th, 2017 and Subtle and Insidious – Technology is Designed to Addict Us written in the *Washington Post* on March 2nd, 2017.

I recommend both.

The concluding lines in the *New York Times* article made me seek out the *Crackdown* passage above. It's where Vinny ditches his smart phone and goes for Sam Spade office décor.

All good literature stays with us in one way or another and it can be triggered months or years later. It's what separates the good novel from the forgettable ones. The New York Times suggests that, "There should be times of the day where it looks like the 1950s or where you are sitting in a room and you can't tell what era you are in."

The article also reminds us that finding time to be in natural environments is a good priority to have. For those of us lucky enough to be living in Thailand those times and places present themselves in various spots. One need only seek them out.

The New York Times and *The Washington Po*st offer some good advice. As does Vincent Calvino. I hope you find a nice natural environment where you can enjoy *Different Drummers – Bangkok Beat Redux.*

CHAPTER 3

The Closing of the Original Checkinn99

I t was a family affair. That is what has made the news so hard to accept for many, that Checkinn99 the basement cabaret bar located between Sukhumvit Soi 5 and 7 since 1957, has been forced to close its doors on the hidden gem of a location today: July 1, 2016. Chris Catto-Smith and his wife Mook took over the establishment on April 1, 2011 when it still employed over thirty hostesses, and cigar and cigarette smoke wafted up to the black and moldy ceiling.

Many were hoping the news of their lease not being renewed was a joke, only to learn that it's part of a serious trend in Bangkok. Chris and Mook spent over 1,000,000 baht on renovations, and business has been booming, thanks both to their legion of faithful patrons located in Bangkok, and their visitors passing through from all over the world. Some well-publicized awards from Trip Advisor and tourists, generally relying more and more on social media than on travel guides, has seen the Bangkok club enjoy a resurgence in popularity of late, bringing it through good times and bad.

The club has a colorful history predating the height of the Vietnam War when it was known as The Copa. USO show entertainers such as Bob Hope, Bing Crosby, Dean Martin and Raquel Welch made appearances at this getaway place of relaxation. Later on, David Bowie would stop by and make friends. More recently, Sammy Hagar has been known to show up straight from the airport to take in the campy ambience positive vibes.

As Chris Catto Smith says, "If I was trying to describe Checkinn99 on a business plan, no one would accept it, but somehow it all comes together."

After a long history of being a private club for Danish members — complete with a dwarf doorman checking credentials in front of the entrance — Chris's tenure revamped the club with live entertainment 7 nights a week.

Gone were the hostesses, but in their place were customers bringing their spouses, girlfriends and mates for a good time, before or after venturing into Bangkok's many other entertainment venues on lower Sukhumvit. The club became female-friendly in a different Bangkok way.

Checkinn99 has hosted two productions of *The Vagina Monologues* since Chris and Mook took over, and has held many other special engagement cultural performances, including *The Rocky Horror Show*, a *Blues Brothers* night and *Moulin Rouge*. The club became known as an arts-friendly place for creative types to hang out — or better yet, to find a gig or discuss a new book idea.

In another against-the-grain Bangkok move, Chris introduced the Sunday drop-in jazz sessions, led by William Wait on saxophone and Keith Nolan on keyboard.

It started slowly from 2:30 pm to 6:00 pm every Sunday and quickly cemented itself as a meeting place for many longtime expats. If you had a new friend in town, an introduction at Checkinn99 was often high on the list of things to do. Some Sundays it was even necessary to get there early to get a good seat.

2016 will also be remembered as the year everyone's favorite Mamasan passed away: Mama Noi, a Checkinn99 original who worked at the club for over 50 years.

And now, not only has the once-recognizable sign been torn down, but all of that history as well.

The move from the old location on the once seamy and now sanitized sidewalks of Sukhumvit has surprised many Bangkok residents.

Here are how some of the city's expat community feel about Checkinn99's fortunes:

"The place is no palace, but what's wrong with that? A little rundown, too funky in some ways. The air conditioning isn't top of the line, but it's real, and there's a real community around it. The place is happening, that's all I can say.

One thing that especially bothers me about this 60-year-old tradition disappearing is that it marks a trend I don't like: the Singaporization of Bangkok. Development these days is mostly ugly, tasteless, and completely ignores old neighborhoods. There's no zoning and virtually no planning, a huge amount of developer greed, and . . . well . . . there goes the neighborhood!" – Peter Montalbano, longtime expat and world-class trumpet player

Another longtime expat who could often be found having a drink in the infamous tunnel leading to the entrance of Checkinn99, is *Bizarre Thailand* author, Jim Algie. He's also currently working with Chris Catto-Smith and British film maker Kaprice Kea on a documentary about the paranormal activity that's been spotted at the ghost-filled club.

The ex-bass player puts it this way, "The demise of the CheckInn99 is symptomatic of what's been happening all over Bangkok recently. We've lost the food street on Sukhumvit Soi 38, large chunks of the Pak Khlong Flower Market, the Rex Hotel, and in the next eight months or so, Cheap Charlie's will be torn down too.

Little by little the city's real character is being eroded in favor of this generic façade of malls, condos, and international chain stores and fast food franchises, which looks like any place and feels like nowhere."

Chris Catto-Smith is an optimist. He believes when one door closes another opens.

As with any good epic story, there is no ending here. Chris and Mook are in negotiations for a new location in Bangkok where family, friends and patrons will continue to feel welcome and make some history of their own.

The new location may not be as funky but it will surely still be a happening place and you can be sure, unlike many other places nowadays, you will feel like you are *somewhere*.

As Chris says, "Those customers are our family. When you have a family, you have a family atmosphere, it's something that, you want to continue. You want to have that legacy long after, individually, you are not here.

And I am sure that what we have created here is going to last, and it's going to last in people's memories, and hopefully in people's lives."

Chris Catto-Smith after a hard day's night
under the portrait of Mama Noi

CHAPTER 4

The Rebirth of Checkinn99

I t's back. From the moment you turn down Sukhumvit Soi 33 for a short 50-meter jaunt, to when you make a left-turn through the arched entryway at the familiar black and white sign you know you are entering the creative world of Chris Catto-Smith's Checkinn99 Bangkok. The seven nights a week live entertainment and events venue, known for its good vibrations, jazzy interior, and tasty tapas, has a kaleidoscopic history both ancient and recent.

Started in 1957 at the former lower Sukhumvit Road location, it had its first heyday during the Vietnam war era and sustained a remarkable run, complete with visiting USO celebrities, dignitaries, spooks, and prominent rock n roll and other stars like Robin Williams hanging out or hiding out among the faithful regulars.

The flood of new developments at times seems to threaten the extinction of the old. Bangkok is not yet a paved paradise, but the trend is worrisome to some long-time residents of the city, as well as tourists who make frequent visits to the *Land of Smiles*. The optimism and perseverance of Chris and Mook blends the old with a newer, larger and much improved home that has long-time customers marveling, and newcomers appreciative. If it's true that everything happens for a reason, the new Checkinn99 on Sukhumvit 33 is a pretty good reason for the closing of the old.

After a couple of pit stops at Sukhumvit Soi 24 and Soi 11 locations, to have a place for their regular clientele to hang out, Checkinn99 has settled in nicely to their new permanent location at an evolving

Sukhumvit Soi 33. There they play a vital role in that evolution, keeping character alive, fighting off the invasion and adding to a more upscale and consumer friendly soi, amidst the rapidly changing Bangkok landscape. The soi once known as, "Dead Artists Street" or "Soi Dead Artists" due to the number of bars named after famous painters long gone, including Monet, Van Gogh, Renoir, Dali and Goya, is now home to live music and events that attract an artistic crowd as well as those just looking for a fun night out. Located catty-corner from Pan Pan, one of the best Italian restaurants in Bangkok, the new Checkinn99, after extensive renovations, occupies the old Christie's bar building. The old Checkinn99 feel is retained, while replacing the funk and junk with modern sound equipment, lighting, and flashy red furniture. There is a comfortable seating capacity of 200 people.

Checkinn99 is an any day or night of the week destination for many, but the Sunday lineup is now a three scoop treat of a day. Sundays start at 2:30 pm at Checkinn99 with their time-tested fan favorite, the Jazz Jam. Led by the William Wait quartet, which has William, a former Psychologist at Fort Help Counseling Center in San Francisco, playing his custom Yamaha alto saxophone. The quartet is filled out by Muk on guitar, Tor on drums and Mai on bass. Being a licensed psychologist is an asset, as William also plays the role of coordinating the many talented musicians that drop in to play on any given Sunday. The level of the revolving talent includes world class musicians and singers, as traveling professional jazz musicians know that Checkinn99 is the place to play and be on any given Sunday. One of those drop-in regulars is Bangkok expatriate and former professional trumpet player, Peter Montalbano, who said:

"The new CheckInn99 is fast becoming a Bangkok treasure, MUCH better than the old location; the funky feeling is still there, but with a lot more class . . . well worth being a favorite hangout for a lot of us. You know who you are."

Bangkok based author and essayist Christopher G. Moore is one of the many regulars that may be found at the Sunday Jazz jams or as part of his unappointed rounds during the Bangkok night. He often brings visiting guests with him for the afternoon. Christopher said of the Phoenix-like rebirth of Checkinn99:

"CheckInn99, I thought we were gonna lose you. I'm glad you're back in the game, the noir Bangkok night wouldn't have been the same without you." Christopher G Moore, author of the Vincent Calvino Crime series.

Following the jazz jam Kevin Wood, a career singer, guitar player and entertainer with an impressive resume, takes over the reins to play from 6:30 to 8:30 p.m. Kevin also serves as artistic and creative director for special events. Kevin penned a Moulin Rouge-like musical called *The Patpong Opera,* which is in the works for a Checkinn99 debut, and was the musical director for the run of *The Rocky Horror Show* at the previous Checkinn99.

Chris Catto-Smith has passed the management reigns to well-known musician and entertainment entrepreneur Keith Nolan. Keith also brings his talent to the stage each Sunday night with a rich mixture of lively blues and rock with his band Cotton Mouth. He's often joined on stage by visiting musicians and entertainers. Over the past few months, Checkinn99 has become a favorite hang out for Australian music doyen, Deni Hines, who, with her husband / manager Daniel, has made Bangkok her home. Deni often joins in the jazz or blues lineups as a guest singer, performing songs she is co-writing with Keith Nolan. Checkinn99 has gone more rock, jazz and blues lately but the only ones singing the blues are the performers, not their fans.

The Checkinn99 tradition has been reborn as a different entity at its new Bangkok location, and it's a venue well worth checking out.

11 Points of Interest on the History of Checkinn99

1. During the shooting of the movie, "Good Morning Vietnam", Robin Williams held court at Checkinn99 often. The old bar is seen as a backdrop in several of the night time scenes.
2. A 4'10" dwarf named Sumai worked in front of the club on Sukhumvit Road as a doorman for many years.
3. One of the owners of Checkinn99 in the late 1970s was murdered in the infamous tunnel that led into the club. The crime remains unsolved.

Keith Nolan at the new Checkinn99 on Soi 33
(Photograph by Ken Sieczkowski)

4.   In 2014 the iconic sign out front, now depicted at the current venue as a Chris Coles painting, was removed by Police order to give more headroom for bicycle riders on the Sukhumvit sidewalk. The bicycle path was never used.

5.   Sammy Hagar once came straight from the airport to Checkinn99 and called Jimmy Page on his cellphone while the band was playing a Led Zeppelin song that Jimmy had written.

6.   The original name of Checkinn99 was the Copa. It was one of the first two-story buildings on Sukhumvit Road. The Copa was built on the site of the old Bangkok ice works established by Nai Lert, with an old ice cellar dating back to 1890's being discovered during renovations.

7.   TripAdvisor named Checkinn99 one of the Top Twenty Hidden Gems in the World for four consecutive years.

8.   A Bangkok Night of Noir literary event at Checkinn99 featured authors Cara Black, John Burdett, Christopher Moore and Dean Barrett.

9.   One of the most successful evenings at the club was the performance of Eve Ensler's *Vagina Monologues.*

10.   The interior of the bar had numerous movie and television scenes shot there, including most recently *The Last Executioner* directed by Tom Waller.

11.   Checkinn99 was the home for the famously beautiful and much missed hostess Mama Noi, who worked as the mamasan in the old club for over fifty years and passed away in 2016. A portrait of Mama Noi hangs near the entrance to Checkinn99.

To get to Checkinn99:

1.   Take the BTS to Phrom Phong Station and walk to Sukhumvit Soi 33. Stay on the left side and it's just a two minutes stroll.

Photo of Kevin Wood by Alasdair McLeod

CHAPTER 5

Interview with Bangkok
Singer Kevin Wood

Kevin Wood is a talented man. I first met him at Checkinn99 four years ago. I got to know him a little bit during a rehearsal for a live starring performance in for the *The Rocky Horror Show*, a production he was also directing. As he admits in this lengthy interview, he is not one for small talk. So we went for big. Mr. Wood has been involved in the music business for over five decades and he has lived to tell some of that tale here today, at *Thailand Footprint*. We discuss the music business, introversion and extroversion, writing, audiences, the idiocy of smart phones, and cockroach infested domiciles among other things:

KC: Hunter S. Thompson famously said, "The music business is a cruel and shallow money trench, a long plastic hallway where thieves and pimps run free, and good men die like dogs. There's also a negative side." I want to get to the negative side, but not yet. Tell me about your career highlights in the music business from the time you were just a frisky kitten to recent times when the whiskers turned a whiter shade of pale.

K Wood: The music business is indeed cruel and unforgiving, and you have to be strong and know how to keep a smile on your face when you're hungry, broke, living in cockroach infested accommodation and the only thing to keep you going is an attentive audience and the sound of their applause… of course this is also why alcohol and other mind altering substances often come into play. It's a roller-coaster ride with lots of lows and some tremendous highs.

As you said, we can get to the low points later. As for the highs, well, I've had quite a few in my 50 years in the business, but some in particular stand out.

The first time was when I was just 17 years old. I was playing in a group called the Gripping Effect. They were considered the best band in our local community, and I was elated just to get the job as the lead singer. We played Soul music, Otis Redding, Wilson Picket, Sam and Dave, the Temptations etc. We got ourselves an agent and played regular weekends but the highlight came when we were booked to do (what we considered a big event at the time) an outdoor gig in a marquee that held 300 people. The only problem was that the star attraction was a famous Trad Jazz musician called Humphrey Littleton so, being a young Soul group, we felt like sacrificial lambs to the slaughter. However, by the end of our set the house erupted, and we were encouraged to do an encore, and again the audience screamed for more. By the end of our third encore Humphrey Littleton's manager had pushed past my crying mother and my beaming girlfriend, and was verbally attacking my father. He thought he was our manager, and was telling him, in no uncertain terms, to get his bloody group off the stage and make way for the star. Whilst this went on, the audience screamed for more, so we obliged with our 4th encore. Eventually, by the end of that, we had to stop, as HL's manager was yelling at us and threatening to physically pull us off the stage. If that in itself wasn't a tremendous enough high for 4 teenagers relatively new to the business, we then spent the next hour signing autographs, and took great pleasure in noting that HL's performance got a lukewarm reception.

More highlights followed, but the next big one was to last 4 years. In the late 70's I was lead singer with a group that had been doing very well for some time. Though at first we declined the offer to become the backing band for the ex-60's pop star Wayne Fontana, we finally succumbed to the offer of more money, bigger gigs and better opportunities. Over the next 4 years we played almost all the biggest concert halls in the UK including the Hammersmith Odeon in London, Glasgow Apollo, Brighton Dome and many more, as well as touring Germany (where Wayne was still considered a big star, and consequently we were treated royally). We became stars overnight, taken to the best places where everything was free, and when I say everything I mean… *everything*. But for me one of the great joys at the time was getting to work, and become friends with, many of the big stars whose photographs I'd had plastered all over my bedroom walls when I was kid.

In the mid-80s I was working in Singapore with my English band when my keyboard player and I were approached by a local Chinese/Singaporean drummer to form a band which would include a Filipino female singer and 2 Malay/Singaporean musicians, making it the first Eurasian band in Singapore. We accepted the job, and almost from the start we became very successful, and were voted best group of that year in Singapore (1985). We got a great deal of press, worked on TV and radio and I couldn't go to the local shop without having to sign an autograph or two on the way, but the biggest moment came when we played the open air Police Academy Concert.

We arrived early for the sound check and noted that only a couple of hundred people were scattered around the enormous grounds so we adjourned to the dressing rooms to relax and have a beer, thinking the event was going to fall flat, only to find that by the time we went on to do our show a few more people had arrived… fifty five thousand, to be exact. When I saw the crowd my legs turned to stone, and the only way I managed to climb the stairs to the stage was because my mind was completely focused on trying not to throw up, and soil my pants at the same time, but the audience were with us from the first few chords.

I can tell you, in all honesty, there is nothing better than holding an audience in the palm of your hand. It's even better than the best sex you could have. What made it even better was making the front page of the Straits Times the next day; just me in the corner of the picture with my arm raised in a fisted salute and 55 thousand people doing exactly the same.

There have been quite a few highlights since then, such as singing with Bangkok's 72 piece National Symphony Orchestra, or singing My

Girl with the Temptations but I think I've blown my own trumpet long enough.

KC: Let's talk psychology. It's one of many licenses I don't have so why not? Specifically introversion and extroversion. How do these two traits play a role in your performances, and in your preparation as a musical artist? Put another way, how do you use introversion and extroversion in your art and in your life to your benefit?

K Wood: Difficult question... I suffered a childhood trauma when I was 6 years old that made it very difficult for me, and although I wanted to be the center of attention (like most kids) I tended to keep to myself, just to stay out of harm's way. This made me an introvert who enjoyed his own company. Then when I was 12 years old The Beatles hit the music scene and I burst out of my shell with a vengeance, only I actually had to learn how to be an extrovert. Once I got the hang of it I enjoyed it, so over the years I've developed a kind of Jekyll and Hyde personality, but these personalities are both very real and very me... I think.

As a singer, I think it's important to do the music you like best, because, as with everything, what you like to do best is usually what you do best, but I think of myself as an entertainer first.

An example of the two opposing traits is; when I was younger I had my own back stage mantra; the introvert in me was a nervous wreck who desperately wanted to crawl back under his isolated rock, so to force out the extrovert I would repeat to myself, "The audience is a multi-headed monster, and you have to go out there and kill it, or, sure as hell, it will kill you." So once I'd psyched myself up, I'd go out there, guns blazing and taking no prisoners... except maybe the cute chick with the low cut top and cheeky grin.

As a writer there have been various reasons for writing my books, but an audience was always there, to a lesser or larger degree. I see no joy in doing it if you can't share the joy with other people.

Art, on the other hand, for me, can't be anything else but introverted, yes I want other people to like my work, but art has to be introverted, or you're lying to yourself and the public.

KC: Sticking with personalities, can you describe the various types of audiences you have had in your five decades in show business?

K Wood: Well, it would be easier to describe the kind of audiences I haven't had.

Apart from doing my party piece for mum and gran I guess my first audience some neighborhood friends. My older brother acted as my manager, and tried to extort money for my performance. I sang Emile Ford's "What do you wanna make those eyes at me for", acapella, which resulted in a swift mass exodus of said friends, and I think my cat attempted suicide because it couldn't get out. I was 9 years old at the time.

Since then I've played to almost every kind of audience there is, including, some of the more notable; the Queens Guards in London, patients and nurses of a Mental Asylum near Manchester, Strangeways Prison in Manchester, British soldiers stationed at Bergen-Belsen (formerly a Nazi concentration camp) in Germany, and several members of the Thai Royal Family.

I've performed to very large audiences in football stadiums and concert halls, and I've performed to as few as 2 people in a small club, but, as they say, size doesn't matter. In fact some of the best shows I feel I've done have been to an intimate crowd in a small club. Queen Bee in Sukhumvit 26 is a fine example, performing with a couple of musicians whom I like and respect (Ted Lewand and John Branton) to regular customers who pay attention and get involved in the performance and allow and encourage us to be adventurous and go off the rails. That's a blast. On the other hand the worst audience I ever performed to was Strangeways Prison; the audience paid us no attention at all and we were a very visual and excitingly insane rock/pop band that incorporated many stage changes and pyrotechnics. To cut a long story short we could have all committed ritual hara-kiri on stage and the only reaction we would have got would have been from an angry janitor who had to clean up the blood afterwards.

Nowadays the cell phone is the curse of all musicians; there's nothing worse than performing to a bunch of ignorant, zombiefied, people who neither know nor care if you are even there; I simply can't get my head round it, why would anyone go to a live music bar with their friends, then all of them spend the evening staring at their phones?

KC: How important is the audience to the performance? Can you perform well to a bad audience and conversely can you bomb in front of a great audience?

K Wood: To me audiences are extremely important. It's a two way street, it's like making love; you give the best you can give and if they do the same it's gonna be a great night, but if they don't, well, you might as well stay home and play with yourself.

For me applause and reaction spell satisfaction. A great audience usually makes for a great night, even if I'm off form, but there have been times when things have gone badly wrong; usually equipment failures, vocal problems, the bass player being fall-down drunk, or, the girl singer has just broken up with her boyfriend who, as usual, is a member of the same band.

The trick for me of doing a good gig in front of a bad audience is just to let it go and have fun with the guys in the band. Of course sometimes that's not easy because you don't like the guys in the band, because the bass player is fall down drunk, the girl singer, etc.

KC: In addition to being a singer and musical performer you've also written a number of books and you are a visual artist as well. Tell me about these art forms. What do you get out of them that you don't get out of singing and performing in front of an audience?

K Wood: As a singer/entertainer I enjoy making people happy, making them laugh and even making them cry; for all the right reasons of course, but it's a sequence of passing moments and all the things you do in those moments flash by 'warts and all'. They can't be changed. You can't say, "damn that was bad, or good, let's do it again"… it's gone. This is why I prefer to write E-mails rather than speak on the phone. The same applies to my writing and my art; I *can* do it again, I *can* trash it if I think it's bad and I *can* keep it if I think it's good.

KC: What books are you most proud of?

K Wood: I wrote my first book, *Onist* specifically for my children because I believed it was important for them to know about my upbringing and about their descendants. I re-wrote it 5 times over a period of 12 years till I was happy with it… or maybe just sick of rewriting it; at Art College I was taught that art is never finished, you just have to know when to stop and move on.

My second book, *Opium Sparrows* was about my personal experiences living in Bangkok and working as a singer, Radio DJ, and manager of a live music bar in Patpong. I wrote it as a novel and all the names were changed to protect the innocent (me) but it was a very graphic and true account of what I'd seen and done, you could say it's my biggest seller but now I look back at it and think it was way too graphic.

I was commissioned to write another book *Sin, Singer, Singapore* about the music scene back in the 80s in Singapore and my days as a "pop star" there, note the inverted commas; the jury is still out on that one.

I had no intention of ever writing a book again, but one day this idea popped into my head and it wouldn't leave me alone; it wouldn't let me sleep at night; it kept poking me when I was nodding off, and if I did get to sleep it would prowl round my subconscious and then attack me with a big stick yelling, "Write me down or I'll eat your children". So in an effort to exorcise the demon, I wrote *The Bougainvillea Bush* (basically it's a love affair between two orphans, a street cat and an ageing, reclusive, disillusioned musician) and, as it turned out, it's the book I'm most proud of. But I only printed 50 copies so I could give it to loved ones and friends and sell enough to pay for the printing costs. Several people have said it would make a great Disney Movie but I'm way too long in the tooth and short in the pocket to chase that carrot.

KC: I'm too big of a Temptations fan to not ask for the back story of singing My Girl with them. What is it?

K Wood: I went to their concert here in Bangkok (11th May 1993) and in the show they asked for volunteers to get up and sing My Girl with them. The person I went with, knowing I knew the song, insisted I get up and, against my better judgment I did.

But there's an interesting back story to the back story.

When big name artists invite guests onto the stage to sing with them those guests are, more often than not, pre-rehearsed plants in the audience as it was in this case; enter me.

It gets better. After the show I left and went to work at the club I was performing in 3 days a week and some hours later a woman, who was a regular customer and knew me, came racing over to me excitedly and, to cut a long story short, she was in fact the organizer of the Temptations concert. She went on to tell me that when the Temptations had seen me heading for the stage they panicked and told her to stop me but she told them not to worry, that she knew me and that I was a pro.

When I'd finished the song Melvin Franklin (an original Temptation) called out to me and when I turned he gave me the thumbs up and said, "Great man" I said thanks and asked him how he was doing he smiled and gave me thumbs up again.

After the concert they told her to come out and find me and join them at the after show party but I'd already left.

KC: You mentioned Queen Bee and Ted Lewand along with the proprietor and musician John Branton. Tell me what those two friends and colleagues mean to you at this stage of your career?

K Wood: The collaboration between Ted and me wasn't intentional, in fact we hardly knew each other when we were asked to form the duo. We weren't even sure we liked each other but were quite sure it wasn't going to work. Nonetheless, we decided to give it a shot and, to our mutual surprise, it did work, and it was a great fun, largely because we didn't think it would work. It worked so well that at one time we were working 6 days a week, until we decided to cut back.

Jump ahead almost four years to Queen Bee and we're now a three piece duo with John on keyboards and I find myself working with two extremely accomplished musicians. Ted is a music teacher and John was a music examiner; there is almost nothing these guys don't know about music. Both Ted and John are great guys whom I have a great deal of respect for, and have fun with.

This is not to say that it's all hearts and flowers. There are times when Ted and I piss each other off. We're not kindred spirits; we perceive entertainment differently, but I guess you could use the old adage that 'opposites attract'. We're often told that we have a chemistry, and that what we do is special. We approach our performance as if we're amongst friends, and for the most part Ted, John and I make a great team.

KC: What do the three of you talk about in the wee small hours of the morning after your gigs?

K Wood: Philosophy, religion, life in general, aches and pains, knife wielding maniacs, and sometimes music.

KC: How important is the wind-down portion of the evening?

K Wood: For me, usually, it's the only time I get to socialize with friends and acquaintances, and I enjoy it very much. I'm not one for small talk but when the alcohol kicks in, people tend to go deeper.

KC: What's the future of live music, specifically for Bangkok.

K Wood: I think live music is reaching its zenith. Gone are the days when people would go out specifically to watch an unknown band. Nowadays people in general seem to see live performances as back-ground music, but the onus doesn't lie squarely on the shoulders of the potential customer; club owners deserve some of the responsibility. There was a time when a club was judged on the quality of its performers. Now it's more a case of, why pay a lot of money for a great show when you can get some relatively decent singer to sing to backing tracks for the price of a couple of beers and a packet of fags, or some wannabes who'll do it for nothing?

In Bangkok it's very difficult for musicians because Thais love familiarity, so any musicians who try to break out of the mold often find themselves without work, extremely under-paid, or playing to an empty house. It's a vicious circle.

KC: Besides Queen Bee what places can you recommend?

K Wood: I don't go out to other clubs (unless I'm working). It's a busman's holiday for me. I now play at Checkinn99 every Sunday after the Jazz Jam. Keith Nolan runs a full program of music there now, so I can safely say you'll be in good hands any day of the week and have a good time there. Be sure and pay your respects to the portrait of the legendary Mama Noi.

CHAPTER 6

New Year's Day: 1960 A Legend Arrives

Written by T Hunt Locke

A young Noi arrives in Bangkok

Her name was Noi. She let her hand slide through the meandering blue water of the Mun River. A reflection glimmered up at her. She did not bother to wipe away the tears that mimicked the river's flow down her cheeks. Sadness had its purpose.

Across the river along the banks the laughter of children playing could be heard. So close yet still a distant land. Kampuchea. Cambodia. A war raged. She knew little of that. It was said her father died fighting there. She knew little of him. Distant memories much as the frivolity of those young children would become. A distant memory to be harbored within a sad present.

Noi longed to be ugly. "Beauty is a curse," she had yelled at her mother only the night before.

"Perhaps," her mother said, pointing a crooked finger at her daughter. Bent from years of toil in the fields, there was little sympathy in her voice. "But you are little use to me in the fields. The men lust. Too much creeping around like lost dogs. And they are poor and worthless. You can make money with your beauty in the city. That is of use."

Those were the last words on the matter. A rusty dilapidated tractor had dropped her off at the river's edge at the break of dawn. "Bus come soon," Noi was told. And so she sat. Not knowing what lay in store. The children's laughter from across the river brought solace. At least she had a distant memory. And that alone was enough to give way to a smile.

And it was that memory, that smile, which would lead her into a new and very different world.

A very different world indeed, Noi thought as she nudged herself out of a daydream.

The rain whipped along the muddy and densely polluted canal. An empty Coca Cola can noisily rolled to and fro along the water taxi's rusted deck. Noi barely noticed. In any case, it wasn't worth her attention. Her destination, as it had been for more than a year, was New Phetchaburi Road.

If the commute had become routine, tonight would be different. A new club had opened. That meant a new mamasan, a new boss, more money. This was good. Still, she disliked change. The words of her mother constantly rattled in her mind. "You can make money with your beauty in the city. That is of use." And she had. Most of the money was sent back to the village, so she felt surprise and sadness at how she was received by her mother on her increasingly rare returns home. Her mother was succinct.

"You stay in the village and eat my food while you should be in the city and earning money."

Still, she had an undying attachment to both her family and village. The laughing children, the mystical flow of the river, and the sweet smell of tamarind, clung closely to her senses. She would return, return with money in her pocket, to build a house, and to rescue her mother from a life of labor.

But that was for the future. Her tattered raincoat was her only defense against the rain. She kept her head low, tenaciously gripping the frayed edges of a scarf which served to guard her latest hairdo. She thought it looked odd. All the girls, her friends, her rivals, competed to have the latest style Hollywood had to offer. She preferred the simple style of the village. These thoughts were unhealthy. At least her co-workers thought so. "Noi, you talk too much of your village. Your life is here. Why live in the dream?" They were right. But, for her, the dream got her through each and every dreary day.

"You, over here," a crass voice called.

The sound of the voice immediately alerted her as to who the club's owner was.

"Now, up on stage!"

And Noi now knew the identity of the mamasan.

She quietly obeyed.

The routine was the same at every club. She would dance on the music-less stage while an aged dour faced lady and squinty eyed Thai man of obvious Chinese descent greedily ogled her. There were two types of girls, one to sit at the bar and hustle drinks and the other to grace the stage. Noi knew her place. She was center stage, the main attraction.

The Starlight had become Noi's home. It was a step up from the previous venues where she had plied her trade. More money was flowing home to Ubon Ratchasima yet she drifted farther and farther away. Even so, the laughter remained. The months peeled away quickly.

The class of foreigner, farang, had improved as well as the rate of pay. She held center stage at the number one nightclub in town. None of that really mattered. For Noi had discovered something wonderful and strange. A crazy little thing called love.

She read the letter over and over.

Dearest Noi,

Not a day goes by where I don't lay in my cot and stare endlessly at your photos. The Kodak I cherish most is the one where we are

*standing by the river in your hometown. Thai New Year was magi-
cal. The fighting here continues to be rough. But don't worry about
me. I'll be careful to stay in one piece and be back to Bangkok. The
only thing that keeps me going is the thought of your embrace and
that crazy little thing called love. I hope this little bit of money
makes your life easier. Forever and with a kiss,*
   Donald

She was careful to neatly fold the letter back up, place it back in the
envelope, and return it to her handbag. Noi clutched the leather purse to
her heart. It was the first gift Donald 'Eli' Whitney had given her. Her
English had improved. But she still could read little.

Not all the foreigners that frequented the Starlight were soldiers. She
had made a friend. A kind man. Sheldon Hancock. He was a writer of
some sort though she wasn't exactly sure exactly what he did. It didn't
matter. Sheldon had read her the letter. Often. But by now she had
memorized it. More importantly, he had helped her to write a reply. Noi
poured her heart out. Sheldon certainly must be a good writer, Noi
thought, because her words did look beautiful on the paper.

"Ten minutes, Noi," one of the bartenders shouted into the
backroom. Another night, another show. She closed her eyes and let her
mind wander back to that time Donald fondly remembered.

"Noi," a voice excitedly shouted.

"What," she answered jumping off of her seat. Perhaps Donald had
returned. Her friend, Meow, would be the first to alert her.

Meow jumped up and down. "Tonight the high soldier come to visit us!"

"Oh," Noi answered somewhat disappointed.

Meow understood Noi's disappointment. Her sister in the bar had
realized the 'Dream.' A kind boyfriend with money, the type who could
take a poor girl out of this life, build a home, go to America. Yes, that
was the 'Dream.'

Meow chided her anyway. "Do not be this way, Noi. One night Donald Duck, the nickname Noi's friends preferred to Eli, will walk through
that door. And he will put you on his wings. But tonight you must be
happy for the other 'dream.'

Noi knew Meow was right. One night with the 'Big' soldier was worth a month with the soldiers Donald referred to as grunts. More money back home. She put on her red lipstick and a smile, took Meow by the elbow, and walked out of the room and into the lights. Showtime! Little did she know, but it was a room to which she would not return. For soon, as she was to find so often in her life, dreams always come to an end.

You wake up, open your eyes, and you find there is only you. And then, if you are lucky, you move on to another dream.

The Copa was in full swing. The hideaway for the international jet set pulsed like no other venue in Southeast Asia. Sophisticated with just the right amount of naughty sass, the Copa oozed money, celebrity, and more than a hint of cloak and dagger.

Noi had come here only two years before. Escorted from the Starlight by a high ranking United States Government official, she had found a new home. And a new home was what she needed. The Vietnam War had become a personal affair. Donald Whitney had succumbed to war's cruel intent, and had a leg blown off. Noi had received one last letter before he receded into the mists, finding herself once again alone in the world. The tears had dried. But, truth be told, in a time of weakness, they were never too far off.

She adjusted the special black mini dress her most recent lover had bought for her. It was expensive. But Spiro, or Baltimore as he liked to be called, was a man of means. She hated him. He seemed to revel in the war that was raging in Southeast Asia. The war that had taken her Donald. If Donald was an angel, then certainly this man of politics was a devil. It didn't matter. In her mind, she had sold her soul long ago.

Still, the Copa always buoyed her spirits. The band had yet to arrive. Noi and her friends, the trendy well- dressed staff, set up for another night of frivolity. She spotted the shy admirer who had nervously ogled her only the night before.

"Hello," she approached him brightly. "What's your name?"

"Hi, I'm Doug. Doug White," he stuttered.

"Good evening, Doug. What is your pleasure?"

Doug's heart skipped. He wanted to just ditch it all. Buck up he thought to himself and just let his feelings gush out. But he was a public relations man. And he had a client. A big fish.

"Well, first off, Noi, I'd like a gin and tonic. And what would be your drink of choice?"

Noi smiled. Her night was off to a pleasant start. And best of all, Doug had spared her the drudgery of setting up duties. She returned to the table and snuggled close to Doug. Oddly, she could feel him squirm.

Doug readjusted himself on the booth. He raised a glass which Noi cheerfully met. "Perhaps you know of my boss," he suggested.

"Ah," Noi said. She understood the situation. Doug was a 'matchmaker' as the girls liked to say. It was not uncommon. From time to time an underling, one such as Doug, would come in to make an arrangement for one of the girls to meet a man who wanted to avoid the glare of a nightclub setting and the gossip which could ensue. She herself had spent many a night at the famed Oriental Hotel which had been restored to its former glory by Jim Thompson and Germaine Krull, entertaining a high level American politician.

"So you want to make a 'date' for your boss."

A pity she thought. There was the alluring dance of innocence in Doug's eyes. In some ways she could see a bit of Donald residing there. This was a guy she could fall for. But, she knew her place. Doug knew his.

"Yes, well, all you have to do is sit here. Uhmm relax. With me if you like. His name is Bing. He'll come to the Copa tonight with his friend, Bob."

Noi shook her head. She also understood this situation. When Doug mentioned Bing and Bob he did not need to elaborate. The famous Hollywood entertainers had made quite a name for themselves in the City of Angels.

"And what should I call your boss and his friend?"

Doug smiled. Noi was young, vivacious, and stunningly beautiful. She was also clever. Noi knew how to play the game. These were the qualities that had made her such a hot commodity with the cloak and dagger State Department bigwigs. It was how she had come to the attention of Bing.

"Bi and Bo will work fine."

CHAPTER 7

Interview with Author J.D. Villines
and Review of Dead Bangkok

Joel Villines is a traveler, a father, a writer, an author, and the owner of a boxing gym in L.A. to rattle off just a few attributes. Other descriptions one can attach to him are more interesting. It is said, on his Amazon author page, that Joel was born at home on a pile of newspapers on Chicago's South side, where he led a truly remarkable life that involved freezing temperatures, reading stacks of books, and accompanying his grandfather to neighborhood bars to play Donkey

Kong. He survived Catholic Schooling, and vowed that if he lived long enough, he would move to a warmer climate. Forty-plus years later, he is finally living the dream, along with having the odd nightmare about ghost-writing a horror screenplay. J.D. Villines now resides in Los Angeles, where he runs Echo Park Boxing and Muay Thai Gym, located on Sunset Boulevard, no less. He also writes for the Hollywood crowd. Before that he spent a lot of time in a stagnant, malaria- filled village on the border of Thailand and Cambodia. If he hasn't been interviewed before, someone screwed up.

KC: Your first novel is a zombie thriller called *Dead Bangkok*. What's the back story on how that evolved?

JD: I was living with my girlfriend (Nok from *Dead Bangkok*) in her village and a few incidents occurred that led to that book. For one, we had just come back from a long trip to Koh Chang, and were spending our days hiking into Cambodia through a little border checkpoint near her village. Not sure exactly how I caught this particular fever but it was a doozy. There was a major monsoon at the time and her family only had a scooter—so they claimed there was no way to get me to a hospital with the dirt roads now being washed out and all. A village "doctor" came by to check on me. He gave me Tylenol and not much else. I had a 106 degree fever for about 6 days straight, and was pretty certain I was dying. I wrote out my "will" which ended up being the first few lines of the novel. *"Ours is a long slow suicide. Life metered out in milligrams and bullets. Parasites and hosts. An ecosystem of the absurd."*

When my fever finally broke, I was physically destroyed but had enough mental strength to demand a ride to a hospital. Somehow they found a cousin with a pickup truck and they took me to a government hospital in Sisaket. They gave me a bag full of drugs and I went back to my girl's shack, slept on the floor under the mosquito net, and wrote the rest of that novel.

Nok – who was my muse at the time and a character in the book, is still my friend, but we are no longer a couple. Her whole family was into some "dark Buddhism" or what we, in the west would call "black magic".

Black magic is generally defined as being selfish in origin. Casting spells for love, money, power, or sex. Maybe a few curses on your business rival as well. I learned about Thailand's huge pantheon of ghosts from her. Actually, the amount I learned about Thailand's underbelly from her was staggering. She was, and is, a total character of a person. I really miss those days in our shack—fever and all.

KC: What have you learned so far during your time on the planet? The important stuff and the unimportant stuff – break it down for me.

JD: A magician's only real power is causing synchronicities to happen. Once you can achieve that—all of the strange, beautiful things in life will jump out at you. Everything else is trivial and not worth mentioning. As of now, I am only adept in my one-man-esoteric order. I still can't afford grimoires bound in human skin but I am saving up.

KC: Talk about aggression: in music, in writing and in the ring. When is aggression most useful to you? When is it most harmful?

JV: You don't need aggression. You only need lack of fear, and an inner-calm. The fearless can move through the world effortlessly. The fearless can defeat any opponent. This is the way of the sage.

KC: What are the cultural differences between rural Thailand and urban USA. Put another way, what are the differences between *La La Land* and the *Land of Smiles*? Contrast your life in rural Thailand with your life now as the owner and instructor of a Muay Thai gym in historic Echo Park, California.

JV: In rural Thailand (Kantaralak, Sisaket), I lived in a shack, swatted mosquitos, and pondered the stars with a girl I loved. In Los Angeles, I live in an apartment one block from where the Black Dahlia was murdered, observe the cult members that permeate the area, and watch police helicopters with a girl that I adore. I came back to the States, ostensibly, to make money so that I could return to live in Thailand one day. Now, I am not so sure that is my goal anymore. There is something to be said for dating an intelligent, successful woman here in the USA. My needs have changed….for now anyway.

The Muay Thai gym I opened is a community gathering place in Echo Park. Very happy to see what it has grown into. The twenty years I spent going back and forth to Muay Thai gyms allowed me to be where I'm at; an entity beyond me. Something that helps spread the Thai cultural meme to people who had no previous exposure to it.

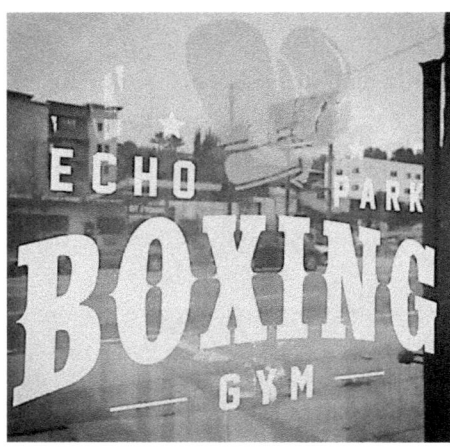

KC: Had any good nightmares lately? Share.

JV: Well, I had been ghost writing a bit when I came back to the States. My nightmare seemed to evolve out of that experience. In the nightmare, I was hired to take over writing duties on a horror screenplay. The previous screenwriter had died while writing it. I will kind of leave it there because I am working it into a story now--but it scared the shit out of me.

KC: What superstitions do you have? Inside or outside the ring.

JV: I seem to constantly find nails on the street, in parking lots, or near cars. I have picked them up for years. I can't even remember how many. Possibly several hundred by now. I get a flash that someone will run over them and then blow their tire out on the highway. So, I pick them up to avert death and disaster. I am aware that the agents of fortune are using me as a tool for good or ill. I could be saving the next Pulitzer winner, or maybe even helping a bank robber get away from a crime. Who knows? I do it anyway.

KC: Lets do some free association. I'll throw out some words and you write whatever first comes into your mind:

Conformity: I do it everyday, and then spend the day undoing it.
Dregs: Some of the most interesting people you'll ever meet.
Drag Queens: My GF lives two blocks from a cross-dressing evil-clown bar. Sometimes they carry axes. The world needs more of that.
Ghosts: I've created my own poltergeist. He goes with me everywhere. So do a few 'hitchhikers' I've picked up in the sundry parts of Thailand.
Breast implants: They look better on ladyboys than real women.
Henry Rollins: He is revered in Redondo Beach where I lived for 15 years—so it's almost sacrilegious to speak against the pontiff of punk. I went to one of his spoken word gigs in Chicago when I was a kid and he ranted about how stupid boxing was (I was a boxer and was kind of like, huh?). Then he proceeded to extol the virtues of lifting weights. Kind of the alpha-bro of the art world. Henry and Danzig should have a morning workout show. I liked Ron Reyes of Black Flag more.
Jerry Brown: His aura smiles and never frowns....his suede denim secret police will come for your uncool niece.
Raging Bull (The movie): Quite possibly, the most unrealistic boxing choreography in movie history. Great movie, nonetheless.
Las Vegas: Where do you start? It's pre-apocalyptic that's just screaming to be post. All you can eat sushi, machine-guns, legal brothels, cheap apartments, and chances are you'll run into someone you know there. The downtown area is trying hard to attract hipsters. I think there's like two or three there now. Considering getting a weekend place there with my GF because she works on TV shows.
Money: If I can eat what I want, and travel when I want—then I have enough.

Steroids: That's a Tim Sharkey Question.

Tanning salons: They are dying out…I hope.

Tattoos: I'm heavily inked. I like most of what I have. The only ones I don't like are the ones I did on a budget. I've yet to get any Sak Yant tattoos, but it's on my list. If I have any room left.

Superman: Least favorite. Totally unlikeable character. He can literally do everything. Batman is just a dude who knows martial arts. Much more easy to relate to that.

Woody Allen: Loved *Midnight in Paris*. Wish he would do a horror movie.

KC: Which writers were/are your mentors? If you don't like that word, tell me which writers you respect?

JV: Philip K Dick, William S. Burroughs, and Hunter S. Thompson were huge influences on my world view growing up. As a kid in Chicago, we didn't have television—but our apartment was full of books. My mom is a beatnik writer so her book selection was top notch. Lately I've been reading *Maldoror*, by Comte de Lautreamont, and a lot of esoteric gnostic stuff as research for my next book.

KC: What is the difference between writing for television and writing fiction for readers?

JV: A lot of TV writing is just trying to keep people's attention. Unless it's Twin Peaks, not many people will stick around for the slow burn development of characters. If you write comedy--it's a lot of one-liners and setups for jokes. For police type shows, it's being edgy without being corny or cliched.

KC: What do you see in your crystal ball?

JV: Souls will reincarnate inside artificial humans, clones, or even computers. We will shed this meat vessel and hopefully move beyond our biological programming. It's all part of a trans-humanist agenda.

You're an atheist, you say? Fear not. They'll find a use for your soul too. There will always be room in the robot brothels on Soi 6.

KC: Damn.

Book Review of DEAD BANGKOK

By J.D. Villines

Are you a fan of GG Allin? Are you more likely to read Mike Fook than John Burdett or Lawrence Osborne? Do you remember how Chris Rock understood O.J. and empathized with the Juice? Does your comedic sense of timing go more to Sam Kinison than Bill Cosby? If you answered yes to any of these questions, *Dead Bangkok – A Novel of Thailand* by J.D. Villines may be the apocalyptic Zombie flesh eating ghost thriller that you have been waiting for your entire life.

As Zombie thrillers go this is the best one I have ever read. I should qualify that I have never read John Russo's *Night of the Living Dead* or *The Walking Dead* series by Robert Kirkman .... or any other walking dead book ever written for that matter. But, hey, everyone has to start somewhere, and there is no better place for a Thailand Zombie ghost thriller than the corroded razer sharp mind of J.D. Villines. His style is not so much like getting a smooth shave as it is watching a hemophiliac try and stop a nose bleed. Villines delivers his prose with the tat tat tat of a Craftsman nail gun bought outside your corner 7/11 store from a perfect stranger.

As our story unfolds an outbreak of brain parasites has turned the living into flesh eating cannibals. Our protagonist, Joel, is a manly man who longs for the days when there were no bills to pay and "A man's worth would be measured by how well he could swing a machete." He gets his wish and then some. There are Conan poses to be made and at least one war cry to whoop. Along the way he also gets to throw some grenades, expensive Molotov cocktails, and one well hardened turd of his own meditative making.

Nok is Joel's Thai girlfriend who is along for the adventure and their relationship is a joy to read about as the expat from California tightropes that fine line between love and hate, talking his Tarzan Thai and making his Tarzan love. The reader can tell Joel does care about Nok, despite his homicidal tendencies. "I had wanted to kill many people in Los Angeles, for no other reason other than that they irritated me." Of course who hasn't had the following thought going on in Joel's drug fueled synapses if you have ever been in a relationship of any length, "My mind was flooded with thoughts on how to kill her." At one point Joel offers Nok some kind advice, "Honey, if something bad happens; kill yourself okay?"

Joel notices that the best defense against Zombiehood is to be in a perpetual state of drug and/or alcohol intoxication. This explains the pockets of life existing in Bangkok amidst the parasite carrying flesh eaters. It also supports why his new best friend, Vato, a drug dealer has survived although not exactly thrived. Joel is the sharpest crayon in this colorful box of Crayolas. Before the threesome head to Pattaya, (another pocket of the living hung over) they meet up with a lady boy named Esmerelda who has a Paris Hilton transplanted face. She becomes the equivalent of the black guy in a 1970s action movie. We know when the face starts to rot if anyone is going to die next it will probably be Paris Redux. She was fun while she lasted.

When Joel and Vato see a fat woman in big underwear Joel thinks her bra will make the perfect slingshot to be used for humanitarian efforts among the parasite afflicted who have unwisely practiced sobriety. It's a scene I would love to see on the big screen some day, including the attempt at a double leg take down. It turns out, "Fat bitch is a pro wrestler." And we haven't even gotten to Pattaya yet.

The action really picks up once they reach the family town by the sea. Some of it I quite liked such as the frequent shadowy ghosts, some of it a bit too scatological and Japanese for me. Give me Linda Blair and some green projectile vomit; I'm a simple man. Maybe this whole Zombie worm flesh eating genre is an acquired taste, like Vegemite. There's a paranormal government study sub-plot involving a mind altering toupee that also adds to the fun. As another reviewer noted, we could have used more of the Joel / Nok banter, tension and confusion as the writing and humor consistently shone in that arena.

What I absolutely loved about *Dead Bangkok – A Novel of Thailand*, in addition to the ending, is the author uses his considerable imagination to the max and only sprinkles in his knowledge and understanding of Thailand when it adds to the story. As it did frequently with his Thai ghost references. This is a well written tale for fans of the genre. And even if you are not, the brisk pace, macabre humor, and sheer insight into the human mind will keep you turning the page. Go for it, one and all.

There is nothing worse for a reading experience than a book that cannot compete with what you did during a memorable summer vacation. That's not the case here. Thanks to the first time author for the inside look at someone Rick James would have dug hanging out with. *Dead Bangkok* is a super freaky book; the kind you don't take home to mother.

CHAPTER 8

Two Book Reviews: Hunters in the Dark
and *Beautiful Animals*

"What is a bad man?" This is the rhetorical question the Cambodian policeman and central investigator, Davuth, poses his daughter, in Lawrence Osborne's moody and spirit-laden novel, *Hunters in the Dark*, (Hogarth 2015). He then follows a set of clues that will see one American underachiever and one English school-teacher cross paths in a tale of double identities and floating indemnity.  Investigators in Cambodia, first and foremost, pursue cases for their own personal gain without the benefit of much schooling. Davuth survived the history of Cambodia precisely because he comes from peasant stock, yet he wields considerable power over the educated "barangs" that frequent his country for "business or pleasure".

When I first learned that Osborne's latest novel would feature an English school-teacher set in Cambodia I thought, how unimaginative is that? I also thought this will be a far cry from his embezzling, on the lam, English attorney who reinvents himself as the high-stakes playing baccarat gambler in Macao, Lord Byron, in *The Ballad of a Small Player*, a novel I enjoyed very much, written by Osborne and published in 2014 (Hogarth).

But just as the American businessman, Simon, living by the river in Battambang, had come around to the idea of ghosts since living in Cambodia, I've come around to the idea that Lawrence Osborne can write about any character whom he wishes to, because he does it with skill and a nuanced imagination. Robert Grieve is the central character – 28 years old, a career English literature teacher from England. His life, like his present day country, is rather bland and ordinary compared to the East. When he has a bit of drowsy luck at the Diamond Club, after a border crossing from Thailand, his fortunes change forever. I see similarities between the Lord Byron and Robert Grieve characters in Osborne's last two novels: they both assume new identities; interpersonal skills are not their strong suit; neither has any love lost for their former country. They both seem to get thrills they never came close to achieving before; they both wear tailored clothes and enjoy the details of a fine meal. Grieve is not your "cheap haircut, cargo pants wearing English teacher in flip flops". Osborne gets his digs in at this expat "subculture" on more than one occasion.

Osborne's characters and settings are equally superb, be they major or minor. The Scottish innkeeper with a penchant for munitions-themed interior design, I particularly liked, along with the yellow-taped grounds and deer that occasionally get turned to a bloody mist. The Dutch artist painting, while naked, at 3:00 am with two young female models seemed vaguely familiar and believable. Other principal characters are Grieve's driver, Ouksa, the Khmer doctor Sar, and his beautiful young daughter and love interest for Robert – the Paris educated Sophal. She is contrasted nicely with Simon's Khmer girlfriend, Sothea, who brings a semblance of balance and karmic energy to the story. Osborne gives the reader many details of the characters later rather than sooner, which enriches the story at an enjoyable pace.

But it is Cambodia and Osborne's art of observation that ultimately seals the deal. Don't skip a sentence of this atmospheric novel by Lawrence Osborne – you will be cheating yourself. The ending is particularly good, although not flawless, due to a clumsy transfer of a known vehicle. Osborne shows us the best and worst of the human experience. As the narrator observes, while Robert eats at an outdoor terrace on Street 136 in Phnom Penh, "What an easy life it was. Just moments randomly pieced together."

In other words, the exact opposite of what Lawrence Osborne has accomplished in writing *Hunters in the Dark*.

Praise Be To Lawrence Osborne – *Beautiful Animals* Review

Lawrence Osborne has occupied rarefied air in writing spheres since he made a name for himself in New York City over twenty-five years ago. Versatility became a strong suit. His star is shining brighter and rising higher of late since he abandoned the young man's dying game of journalism for the equally risky life of a full-time nomadic novelist. After making it there he acquired or maintained an animal confidence to make it anywhere. He has lived or visited for stretches in Mexico, Istanbul, Macao, Italy, Greece, Cambodia, and Bangkok where he currently resides in a spacious condominium. The odds favor that there is no wind chime hanging above the balcony. His grown son lives in Japan.

The British born Osborne ticked all the right boxes to gain proper employment in London or New York with his Cambridge education and short stint at Harvard but opted instead for a pair of traveling shoes. As expats who choose to live in Bangkok go, Osborne brings more social capital to the scene than your typical foreigner living in Thailand. This is to be admired, ignored, envied or derided depending on your own psychological make-up, accomplishments, time management skills, and views on expat society and social standing.

The class conscious and taste conscious (good and bad) Brit was a veteran feature writer for The New York Times Magazine. He's been published in Playboy, The Wall Street Journal, Salon, The New Yorker, and Men's Vogue where he penned a monthly column on wine. His literary works are represented by Elyse Cheney and her agency. Ms. Cheney made a credible list of the 50 Most Powerful Female Executives in New York City for 2015. Osborne's non-fiction books include, *The Poisoned Embrace*, *The Wet and the Dry*, *The Accidental Connoisseur,* and *Bangkok Days*. Recent honors include being selected by the Raymond Chandler estate to write a Philip Marlowe crime novel. The work has been submitted but no publishing date has been announced. His critically acclaimed novel, *The Forgiven* is now a screenplay to be directed by John Michael McDonagh. In short, life is hard but not right now for Lawrence Osborne.

Beautiful Animals is the third Osborne novel that I have read – *Ballad for a Small Player* and *Hunters in the Dark* the latter set in Cambodia, are the other two. I found similar themes in each, along with decadently descriptive prose. The two main characters are young, fit and beautiful females. One slightly younger and more beautiful than the other. "Beautiful as panthers" according to Sam, short for Samantha, an American on summer holiday with her parents, the Haldane's from New York. The primary setting is the Greek Island of Hydra and the surrounding areas. There Sam meets and falls under the spell of narcissistic Naomi, the dream seeking daughter of a rich British art collector, a hesitant raconteur named Jimmie Codrington. The inevitable island gossip includes rumors that Jimmie once palled around with Aristotle Onassis. Old Bohemians traced back to Leonard Cohen's day still survive. Jimmie has owned an expensive Hydra home on a hill since the 1980s, filled with precious art. The acrimonious household includes Naomi's not quite wicked step-mother of Greek origin, Phaine. Funny, her nickname, is snobbish and not particularly humorous when she's not making a toast or sober. Funny doesn't make the grade compared to the birth mother. They never do.

The novel is billed as a psychological study. It is. It could also be called a psychological simmer; it never gets up to a full boil, but that's probably in the recipe Osborne planned to serve. The story is often dark, in places, but as the languid narrative voice states and this reader agrees, "The dark, however, was not a bad place to be." Had the author heard a different calling he would have made a fine psychologist. A cruel eye makes for a better diagnostician, no doubt, than a confined therapist. People rarely change in Osborne's novels and when they do it's usually not for the better.

There is a resentful maid, of course, a Greek named Carissa who likes to have a laugh at the tourists' expense. Loyal or not is anyone's guess in the early stages. A rowboat oar wielding, pot selling local female makes recurring and memorable entrances and exits. Brief shadows of supernatural beings or guilt are also served up, ambiguously. Thankfully, no short-cuts were taken in the spiritual realm.

Pacing is Osborne's strength yet there are possibly overly descriptive passages that include food and drink of the delicious and expensive variety. There are more feasts than assassins in this tale. Other readers may find the going slow. The story turns early on when Naomi and Sam discover a bearded Arab wearing only track suit bottoms and vagabond thongs. A scheme is devised to help the Muslim migrant for humanitarian reasons. Or not; it's never clear. The secular Osborne must have had fun pairing godly and ungodly people together. Neither is particularly moral, even when overpaying for baked goods. That's the desired message to consider.

Bad things happen to not so good people without a whole lot of action or dialogue going on at times.

The most likable character is a no longer dashing but still refined 70 year old sleuth, Mr. Rockhold. I enjoyed Rockhold for many reasons including his prudent choice of red wine. In Osborne's fictional world the investigator wears a Panama hat (not a Fedora) and politely holds it to one side as he introduces himself to a panicking Naomi. The migrant, Faoud, turns out to be refined and educated as well and has a musical background. He later trades in his sandals for a pair of $600.00 shoes. A mistake, and the chase is on.

If there is a weakness to the storytelling in *Beautiful Animals* it is the believability of the plot points, big and small. Had the manipulative animal been American and the persuadable animal been from England I doubt even the author would have bought into the predicaments that ensue due to poor decision making made by intelligent and affluent people with much to lose. They both, after all, like the reluctant police officers pursuing a dangerous criminal in the tiny Italian settlement of Pian di Sco, cared about their lives, or should have. The fact that the nationalities are reversed does not make the scenarios any more credible. On the plus side before the plot points are made, misdirection and uncertainty are the norm.

There may be some worlds where a father can keep an audible secret concealed from his daughter for thirty years but none that I have been around. Osborne makes up for these lapses with his keen sense of observation and a breakdown of manipulation, apathy, meaninglessness, morality, religion, and greed. These elements coupled with the pacing make this a quick and sinister read.

Beautiful Animals should enjoy brisk sales on the East coast of the USA and with those who have summer homes in desirable locales. Hollywood will also likely take notice. I enjoyed and recommend *Beautiful Animals* by Lawrence Osborne. But, I am looking forward to his take on Philip Marlowe. That should go down a treat. Lawrence Osborne knows that the best way to get a handful of simmering eggs to hard boiled is to turn up the heat.

Beautiful Animals is available at all the usual outlets. Published by Hogarth Press.

CHAPTER 9

Interview with English Gentlemen Author Lawrence Osborne and Review of Only to Sleep

Bangkok based author Lawrence Osborne agreed to meet me for a post-interview, interview of sorts at The Bar Upstairs on Sukhumvit Soi 11. He arrived walking briskly, his Italian shoes pointing up at alternating forty-five degree angles with knees only slightly more bent than a Chinese soldier. The in-demand author has a great laugh and loves champagne, chorizo, and cheese. His eyes roll at times, his head nods quickly and he doesn't do chuckles – you get the full shotgun blast of life from Lawrence. He is kind and caring at times – indifferent to other things. He's a man with his priorities in order or as he put it, "I no longer care." When we parted ways in front of Apoteka, where Keith Nolan and Cottonmouth were soon to be playing, he walked almost as quickly, passing on the many taxis available. I got the feeling he would keep up that pace for as long as he wished – until he had a reason to stop. Some day I may write further about that bubbly night. Until then enjoy this interview we conducted via online correspondence:

KC: Tell me about your mother, please. Specifically how she influenced you in the areas of literature, language, and more generally life.

LO: My mother was Irish, her family from a small island in Clew Bay where they held an O'Malley coat of arms. She grew up in Newcastle and ran off to Rome when she was 19 to become a journalist, in 1953 I guess. She went to Naples and fell in with Lucky Luciano, and meanwhile contracted a lifelong love of Italy and the Italian language – which she passed on to me. In fact, I was sent as a teenager to Florence to stay with one of her friends there and learned Italian the easy way. She may well have passed on the idea of romantic escape or flight – what she did was incredibly bold for a penniless post war girl of 19, when Naples was a pretty wild place. She loved it. I wonder if coming back to England later was an irksome thing for her. Either way, she was a book lover and a radio play writer later (her plays were performed on BBC radio 4). The very idea of being a writer certainly came from her, as did the idea of not caring about success. She was very idealistic about those thing, a high romantic.

KC: You're on a roll right now with a string of well deserved successes. We could discuss those, but where's the fun in that? Take me back to a place and time when your future seemed less sure, dark or even dreary. Where were you and what were your thoughts about your future as a writer at that time? Be positive if you must.

LO: My thirties especially were pretty grim. I was alone in New York, no career to speak of, living in people's front rooms, no credit cards and sometimes about 60 bucks a week to live on. This went on for years, seven years maybe. I almost gave up. I once tried to off myself with a shotgun in a snow bound lodge above Hunter in upstate New York but couldn't do it. Of course, I wasn't really determined. When I was 41 I got a piece accepted by the NY Times Magazine and it all went into reverse. But getting a novel published was yet another saga on top of that – it took another 12 years to get one accepted. It's interesting because I was shut out of the whole thing when I was young but I was able to make a living as a journalist later and at quite a high level in New York. But it was never really what I wanted to do. My novel *The Forgiven* lay around for years because agents wouldn't touch it – I eventually sent it out myself and thank god it was accepted by the very first editor who read it (he was on the Friday train home to New Jersey and offered for it the following Monday). So writing for me was always touch and go. I don't know why it was so bloody difficult – I guess I'm not much of a net-worker and journalism was a worthy diversion for a few years. But ultimately it's a mystery. In my fifties, I no longer cared and that was liberating.

KC: Your move to Bangkok looks brilliant with the aid of hindsight. You couldn't possibly have known matters would turn out so well at the time. It seems risky to me as a distant spectator. Did you have a Plan B for a foreign residence? What made Bangkok, Thailand your first choice? With the amount of traveling you do is Bangkok still your preferred place to reside or are you considering a new chapter and a new place to call home in the near future?

LO: I knew Bangkok would be a good move for me. After 20 years in New York I was exhausted, frazzled, out of cash, with chronic bronchitis and a lot of frustration about wasted time. So after my mother died I was asked by Newsweek to go meet Pedro Almodovar in Madrid and we hung out a bit ; Pedro (an expert in all things motherly) said, "Don't go back to New York. Just keep rolling. It'll be fine." Sound advice! Really, that guy should be a top therapist. I love him. And it turned out to be true. There was nothing to worry about, as it turned out. You get your platform, a room of your own, you settle in and you start working : that's exactly what I did. A novel a year for six years. In the end, it doesn't matter where you are unless it's Basingstoke. And even in Basignstoke you could arrange your platform if you had a mind to. But Bangkok is a great city for a solitary writer. I have few plans to move on as of now.

KC: As of this writing *Only to Sleep* has not yet been published. What was your approach in preparing to be only the fourth novelist to write a Philip Marlowe book? Is it a safe bet that you never read *The Black-Eyed Blonde* by John Banville or *Poodle Springs* and *Perchance to Dream* by Robert B. Parker? Which of the seven Raymond Chandler novels did you read prior to or after your undertaking? Did you read his essay, *The Simple Art of Murder*? Can you comment on that if so?

What other research did you do regarding either Chandler or Marlowe that our readers might find interesting?

LO: I read everything. But then I was resolved not to copy any of it, not even Chandler at his best – because what would be the point of that? I wanted to write my own book. In fact, I think that's the only way to do it. Chandler is a strange cat, and his novels are just as strange – at the very least, I thought I could put forth my own strangeness as a humble offering. I set in the Mexico of 1988 which I knew intimately from working as a journalist there in the early 90's. So at least the setting was personal and first-hand. That was important to creating something new and in some way authentic. It become a reverie on old age, a love poem to rural Mexico, and a few other things, but not a pastiche of 50's Chandler.

KC: You have a novel, I believe, titled _The Kingdom_, which will be about Thailand. Authors are notorious for not wishing to discuss future works so tell me as much or as little as you care to about what readers can expect to find when that book comes out in 2019.

LO: I have to keep mum about it for now, but yes it's a story about four women living in a huge apartment complex around the time of a coup – which one, past or future is left deliberately uncertain. It's quite a Hitchcockian book, and there are no bargirls in it.

KC: What, if anything, have you got against wind-chimes? They seem harmless enough.

LO: I don't mind other people's wind chimes, I must grudgingly admit, but whenever they are too close I think of myself dying for some odd reason – you might want to psychoanalyze that, but I tried to do so and failed. It's one of those things.

A Book Review of ONLY TO SLEEP
A Philip Marlowe Novel by Lawrence Osborne

Two years ago Bangkok based author Lawrence Osborne was put in an enviable and unenviable position. Osborne was given the opportunity to say yes or no to becoming the third author to write an authorized Philip Marlowe detective novel, other than Raymond Chandler. Chandler completed seven novels in the well-known series starting with The Big Sleep published in 1939 and ending with Playback in 1958. An unfinished manuscript of *Poodle Springs* at the time of Chandler's death was found. It was completed by Robert B. Parker and published thirty years later. Parker would go on to pen the first approved sequel of a Marlowe novel, *Perchance to Dream*, published in 1991. Benjamin Black was next handed the baton or stick of lit dyna-mite. *The Black-Eyed Blonde* was published in 2014. *The Black-Eyed Blonde* by Black, better known as Booker Prize winning author John Banville was met with critically mixed reviews and disappointing sales.

Thus a series of choices resulted in the birth of *Only To Sleep*. The Chandler estate had to decide if another sequel was legacy worthy. Lawrence Osborne had to decide, as he writes in the Author's Note, whether to venture into the perilous position of stepping into the mind of not only another writer but one of his characters. Osborne had the luxury of taking his time making that decision. During that period he made three additional choices: Marlowe would be 72 years old, the setting would be south of the Southern California border, and the year is 1988. After that he wrote the first twenty pages. Then and only then did he say yes to the project.

Can you imagine a Marlowe novel written in the Amazon age not being panned? I can't. So if you are looking for book reviews that trash *Only to Sleep* they are out there in spades and some of them are entertaining. But before you opt to do that I recommend that you read the reviews of *Only to Sleep* written by Osborne's peers. Laura Lippman's review in The New York Times is particularly good. Of the people actually capable of writing a Marlowe novel none I have seen have been critical in a mean-spirited way. Quite the contrary. That tells me something. After all, we live in mean-spirited times. Please note: I hated *Lady in the Lake* by Chandler. One of the worst crime novels with one of the clumsiest plots I have ever read. Mr. Chandler did a great job of describing bricks and mortar though. 2 1/2 Stars.

I feel better now.

There are enough Chandler-like sentences in *Only to Sleep* to keep most purists happy, "It was ninety-seven in the shade and there was no shade." "He moved like a sloth in linen." Or "She seemed dressed for a date in the middle of nowhere." Original thoughts but as one question in the tale goes, "What was wrong with clichés anyway? They serve their purpose." However, it is the Osborne sentences that kept me turning the page even when peppered with food, drink, and regional language, specialties of the writer. This is, as the author admits in a published interview, more of an Osborne novel than a Chandler one. If that's a bad thing it remains an unsolved mystery to me.

What *Only to Sleep* gives you that other Marlowe novels do not is an elderly, silver-tipped cane-toting protagonist and a seventy-one year old primary antagonist. The latter is said to be, "The most generous man in the world" and he's a mean son-of-a-bitch too. Let the games begin. And they do, with a vengeance. The spirit of Marlowe past has not been a retaliatory figure merely for the sake of retaliation but that's what we get on more than one occasion. Osborne takes detours from Marlowe's (or is it Chandler's?) psyche with confidence. There is no man with a gun entering through a door at any time. There are no guns or bullets at all. The cane we are introduced to has been used by Marlowe since he broke his foot in 1977. A Japanese "sleeping blade" made by a master smith in Tokyo is tucked inside the elegant walking stick. Marlowe is "Out of the combat zone now." But that has to do with his voluntary surrender on the battlefield of love. The only sexy thing he sleeps with nowadays is his cane. There are no sex scenes of Marlowe with a much younger woman in this story – another good call for the times – but jealousy rears its head plenty. Marlowe is old, after all, not dead. We know or at least we think we know that the jewel-steel blade will replace the Colt Detective Special at some point. But when? There is no sorrow for the reader when a good writer takes his time and Osborne does. A slow simmer gets you to hard-boiled after all. Eventually, the predator in Marlowe is reawakened. His Big Sleep will have to wait.

Mexico and San Diego (headquarters of Pacific Mutual insurance) were old haunts for the author during the 1980s when he was an investigative reporter for a San Diego newspaper and he uses that knowledge well. Mexico and Baja, California are the shining stars here, not the Golden State or Bay City. A bull fight with opera glasses replaces the bar fights and smashed beer bottles of decades gone by. There is a grieving widow to be found, close to forty years younger than her said to have drowned husband. It is here that Osborne's time as an expatriate must have been called upon. "We all need something in this world. We all come from places where we can't get them." That line could be placed in many an Osborne novel and it works perfectly well in this one.

All the characters in *Only to Sleep* are interesting, if not vital. Just as importantly, there were not too many to track. Likewise for the dead bodies. Kill Bill this is not. My favorite moment comes from a misfire by Marlowe using his now fashionable weapon of choice. His days of placing a perfectly symmetrical bullet-hole in a perp's head are over and he knows it. Marlowe has changed since he was thirty or fifty. Why would he not? You may or may not like the changes but recognizing them and hearing his musings on aging should be part of the fun in this read. After all, "You get so tired of the people you already know." I read *Only to Sleep* in three sittings, when it could easily be read in two. Mainly to prolong the enjoyment. As Topper the mystery man who calmly spins tops says, "Likes and dislikes are for little boys." This is a good book to be read by men and women who can give it the non-grudging admiration it deserves.

A paragraph caught my eye around the midway point in *Only to Sleep*:

"So we are forced to read the puzzling code that other men devise for us. I resented it. Who wouldn't?"

Lawrence Osborne has succeeded in doing just that. He has taken a puzzle left to him by a legendary writer. In fact he read the code that his peers Parker and Black wrote as well. There may have been times when he felt forced to do so. It's not the typical research an accomplished author is required to do. But in the end when he looks back on *Only to Sleep* I doubt that he resented it. Why would he?

CHAPTER 10

"The poet knows we are all dying men."

An Interview with John Gartland

Photo by Mark Desmond Hughes
Art by Manual Dane

KC: You're not a young poet any longer but you've been a poet, I suspect, in one form or another for at least fifty years. Fifty years ago it was 1968. What advice would the present day poet, John Gartland give to the poet of 1968?

JG: That twenty-year-old, in 1968 was studying for a degree in English Language and Literature. at the University of Newcastle on Tyne It was a rich and vital training in the world of belles lettres; of great poetry, and works of prose fiction. It also took in, in the first year, a grounding in Anglo-Saxon literature.

I'd first of all applied, the year before, to the University's Fine Art Department (where Brian Ferry had been a student). I did the entrance exams, but failed to win a place. I wasn't much of a painter, though I had sold a few paintings through an art shop in my home town. Following rejection by the Art Department, I'd attended a teacher training college for a year, re-applied to the University English Department and had been accepted.

It was comparable, in literary terms, to the intensive classical training in drawing and figure work that was once traditional for visual artists. I was a kid from the North West rust-belt. Getting to University was a huge break for me. I was pretty much in awe of the literary "Great Tradition", as F.R. Leavis called it. I had some poems printed in poetry magazines on campus, and I was writing poetry in a low-profile way, usually getting feedback on it from my girlfriend, who was also an English undergraduate. There was a poetry fellow position, for a poet who would visit the English Department and offer advice on any creative writing that students were doing. One poet in that role, Basil Bunting, offered me the best advice; to get out and "live some more". I had some talent, but I wasn't ready yet to write anything much of substance. When I was ready, years later, that early training kicked in. Meanwhile, I'd done a score of jobs, and travelled widely. My advice to me in 1968, with benefit of hindsight, would be, have more confidence, and trust that poetic spark. Bunting was right of course. I needed to grow up. I'm still working on that.

I did have a creative alter ego, however. I wrote a weekly satirical verse column, on politics or university affairs, in the weekly student newspaper, Courier. A friend and fellow English student was a talented caricaturist and painter, and we did this weekly verse satire / caricature in the paper, which worked well for a couple of years. My artist friend went on, in subsequent years, to become Wilko Johnson, rock guitar hero, launching, out of Canvey Island, with the Doctor Feelgood band, to international success.

Looking back on it, the weekly pressure to produce a verse column of a comic / satirical nature, to a deadline, was a useful discipline, and it taught me more than I realized, in basic technical skills.

Poetry ID

All those years ago, on Tyneside,
when we'd asked of Paris between the wars,
of Eliot and Pound, and their meetings of course,
and he'd looked at our fledgling poetry;
Bunting said, "It's all right, but live some more.
You need to go out and live some more."
I said thanks, and knew, as I closed his door,
he meant Poetry ID.

I've chauffeured cars and worked in bars,
crossed seas and worked illegally;
crashed out in. Split, swabbed blood and shit
from floors in Vancouver casualty.
I've crossed the Rockies on a train
and jumped by parachute from planes,
drove a Cadillac through the F.M. band
from New York down to Miami.
Met Mozart in Carnegie Hall,
Bix Beiderbecke on Hadrian's Wall,
got woken up by lightning
on the warm South China Sea.
Been there and back, and gone off track,
put the Darren Mountains in my pack,

I've taken stock at Lion Rock,
and swum in Lake Euphoria,
stirred Zen into my tea.

I've known apocalyptic trips
and rolled some monumental spliffs,
I've rocked to Doctor Feelgood's riffs,
been frightened, heightened, free.
I've laughed a lot and loved my share,
I've come round in intensive care,
but many I loved no longer step
the headlong days with me.
I toast their sweet reluctant ghosts,
and all we did together, most
of all, this lush, uncharted coast
of Poetry ID.

Listen; words are the ladder we climbed from the slime.
Words that spring to your lips and sing of your time
are shouts in the throat of antiquity;
old oratory, shrapnel hurled
right out of history.
Magical, fierce, exuberant and sad,
words made us wise and sent us mad.
Rhyme's a trapeze we swing out on;
out over birth, dissolution and death.
Rhyme, old as the breeze, and mysterious as breath.

Look, out as far as you can see,
there's love and birth, magnetic north,
the stars, and Poetry ID.
And I've come as before to the old poet's door,
to pass right through it, as you see.
I greet his shade, then turn once more,

ambiguous, naked, and stubbornly free,
with thanks, and a smile, a fond farewell,
and Poetry ID.

KC: Tell me about the changes you have seen in those fifty years. The Grateful Dead wrote a song titled, "What a Long Strange Trip It's Been" in 1977. Tell me about your trip.

JG: I suppose my equivalent piece to the Dead's "Long Strange Trip" would be "Cantos of Cred.", a fly-over of the dozens of jobs I've done. That's printed later in your book.

As regards social changes, I've seen a crushing growth in the bureaucratization of life, in the UK, where I was born. It has turned into the most snooped-on, over-regulated and politically-correct nightmare. Free speech has been drastically curbed, an imported religious extremism institutionally protected, and democratic freedoms undermined.

However, my personal life-trip from day one took me through many major historical gateway events. I'm seventy years old now. Consider the exponential rate of change over that period.

Socially, there were huge improvements in health care, nutrition and the standard of living. The National Health Service made doctors' expertise and antibiotics widely available. Unemployment was an unknown problem in my youth, and there was the possibility of access to higher education for kids (like me) from working class backgrounds, via selective examinations and grammar schools. I remember that, in my State Primary School, in the early 1950's, we were given pens with steel nibs, to write with. One child had the responsibility of filling our desk ink-wells with black ink, from a large bottle. Shades of Bob Cratchit. (In infant school in 1953 we'd been given special blue souvenir drinking glasses, decorated with the royal coat of arms, to commemorate the coronation of Elizabeth the Second. Exciting, eh?).

My mother was a farmer's daughter from Galway, in the west of Ireland, who'd had little education. She told me that she and her sisters at one time walked to school barefoot. She came over to England to work in a factory in my home town when she was just eighteen. She was supposed to stay with a distant relative, but they'd turned out bad, so she'd had to go it alone. She'd told me semi-humorously years later, that King George VI came to visit the northern town, in pre-World War Two years, passing through in a motorcade. As a green young country girl, she'd had no idea what to expect. "I thought he'd be like fairy people" she said wryly. That was a very different world. My parents met while working in the same factory. My Dad used to say her family in Ireland rebuilt him, after the war, on farm food and Guinness. We went to Ireland, and the farm, every year in my early days. That two week holiday was the high point of the year.

ON JOLLEY STREET

As we walked into Jolley Street together,
you had slowed your customary pace.

Around the old Infirmary,
streets of houses without doors,
windows without curtains. Dust.
Forsaken rooms lay gutted of all private comfort,
and demolition smoke was in our way.
Around the old Infirmary
they were tearing down the terraces.
The old town we were born in, coming down.
It must be more than twenty years. It must!

And you had slowed your customary pace.
And strange, out there on Jolley Street
I didn't read the omens straightaway.

Your soldier's tales had drawn for me
such shattered places.
Anecdotes of war, and close escapes;
your travels, drawn so vividly
on Sunday walks,

across the years, across the town.
The annals of your boyhood days.
Much laughter, up and down, we had!

I was the little boy you entertained,
and you, the storyteller, loved a beer
and books and poetry; my interesting Dad.

Despite your ragged nerves left by the war;
your hands that sometimes shook as if before
that bygone discharge from a military hospital,
in entertaining rambles you'd amuse and you'd delight.
But something unforgotten is the sight of private tears
on those Remembrance Sundays, in our town.
The way you could flesh out their "Glorious Dead";
your mad Welsh chum who'd dance the seven veils,
dispensing army boots, a lousy shirt,
each piece of war-stained kit, in lumbering pirouettes,
each time you'd reach a respite and some wine.
He didn't give a shit
for all the King and Country stuff,
and sang odd bits of opera, like you.
In time the war swept him away,
and many others you would mourn
each time "that bloody trumpet"
(so my mother termed it) blew;
Remembrance Day.

I'd ask my childish questions and she'd stay
beside you, arm about your shoulders,
with her jaw set in that stubborn way;
just hating what the Last Post did to you.
How fierce she was; and Irish, too, those moments;
fighting hard, to keep your marching ghosts at bay.

I'm at the old Infirmary again.
While you're out in a waiting room
the specialist's pronouncing on your case.
Incurable, and far advanced, he says;
precise, discreet.
And though I speculated twenty years about it,
still, I ask if I was right;
as we walked out,
to tell the truth on Jolley Street.

But I had no closer friend than you.
And I, you see, had it been me,
would not have wanted you to lie.

I still can see your face and its emotions;
I still relive the anger
as I watched life tear you down.
Soon after you had gone I felt I didn't
want to see the place we strode about so often.
In any case, with landmarks lost,
what would I recognize about the town?

There was no closer friend than you.
In spite all the other things I'm grateful for,
that's why
I bitterly regret you had to show me,
prematurely, your ultimate example;
how to die.

My area in the North West, between Liverpool and Manchester, was
classic rust-belt, a coal-burning, long heavily-industrialized place, large
chemical factories, caustic soda and soap works, flour mills, steel
processing plants, wireworks, coal mines, box works, aluminium
fabrication, hydraulics factories and gasworks, and many more. There
were always factory jobs available, in student vacations, and I did many.

We used to get regular dense fogs in winter, before the Clean Air legislation was introduced.

The air was bad in that town, very polluted, and I got pneumonia and a collapsed lung when I was three. There mustn't have been adequate emergency treatment available in my local hospital, because I was treated in a special hospital, for chest complaints, out near Liverpool and far from my home. My parents had to take a long bus ride to visit me. They were both working, and their jobs simply did not allow them to take such a long trip often, after work, and arrive in time for visiting hours. I remember being the one child, in a cot, in a ward full of bronchitic industrial workers, and coal miners with black-lung. They were very kind to me, but I developed a real case of separation anxiety from my time there, which left its mark for years afterwards.

The local public library was a favourite haunt of mine. Saturdays in my boyhood meant a trip to the swimming baths, a walk around the town museum, and a change of library books. Walking home, I'd be laughing and joking with my pals, crossing the bridge over the railway tracks to Bank Quay station, by the chemical works, along the River Mersey. Liverpool and Manchester were both about an hour away, by train.

There was the arrival of colour television, Rock n'Roll, the Teddy Boys, the spread of popular musical culture, via records, 45's and LP's, then stereo sound and hi-fi, reel-to-reel tape recorders, then audio cassettes, then videos and CD's etc. Movies developed Cinemascope, dynamic sound, Technicolour, and special effects.

There was the availability of more mass-produced cars to buy, and new roads and motorways to drive them on. It was a golden period of new social mobility, when petrol was cheap, and before speed cameras were thought of, and before the road network clogged up with traffic.

There was the landmark introduction of the contraceptive pill (which unlocked sex), affordable international air travel, (which unlocked the world). Feminism kicked off with Germaine Greer's breakthrough book, *The Female Eunuch*, and liberalization of attitudes grew in many areas, from dress to sexual behavior and the availability of drugs. The outcomes weren't all uniformly good, but they were truly revolutionary to live through.

Then there was the arrival of the photocopier, the fax machine, and cheaper phone calls via the privatization of the telecommunications industry. Satellites in geo-stationary orbit fulfilled writer Arthur C. Clarke's predictions, providing instant international communications, for voice, data and TV. Then came mobile phones, plus the arrival of broadband over old voice networks, then fibre-optic cable leapfrogged the bandwidth of old copper-cable phone networks, bringing new rapid voice and data communication, plus Cable TV. There was also the advent of the Personal Computer, the Internet, and Smartphones.

There was nuclear power, lasers, holography, mass- immunization, unlocking the genetic code, the elimination of polio (a disease I remember had once confined a cousin of mine in an "Iron Lung") the elimination of smallpox, developments in plastic surgery, the availability of cosmetic surgery and organ transplants, and cyber implants, and brain-scans, and new drugs to curtail classical madness.

Rock Around the Clock.

Oh yes, there were also Sputnik, the first orbiting satellite, dogs in orbit, then men (and women) in orbit; first, Yuri Gagarin, circling the globe in a tiny capsule, then John Glenn, NASA's flights and then the moon landings, and the exploration of Mars by robots, and the building of the International Space Station. There was the development and open testing of the Hydrogen bomb, nerve gases and biological warfare. There was the (first) Cold War and the age of M.A.D. There was Rock n' Roll, Bill Haley and the Comets, Teddy Boys, Angry Young Men, Elvis, the Beatles, the Stones, Cream, Blues, Dylan, hash, acid, Reggae, the Korean War, Suez, Viet Nam, jogging, yo-yo's, hula-hoops and Disco. There was the scourge of Aids, the spread of SARS through booming international travel, there was Ebola, flesh eating viruses, mad cow disease, accelerating dementia, and Rap music.

There was the political crucifixion of British M.P. soldier, poet and classics scholar, Enoch Powell, for predicting the future of the UK, memorable assassinations-a-plenty, from the Kennedys to Martin Luther King, and John Lennon, and many, many more. There were endless wars, the rise of militant Islam and the auto-destruction of Europe by demographic conspiracy. We were all expected to worship Globalism.

THE CORPORATION

Lie back and learn to love
the corporation.
Especially on a daily basis
rape means rage and tribulation.
Get wise that such humiliation's
futile and corrosive;
not to mention an explosive parcel
ticking in your sanity.
You can't reject the corporate embrace.
To think you can resist
is merely vanity.
Understand, you're on your back,
my friend,
and they're right in your face.
It's macro-economic systems
goosing all humanity.

True, the world's in corporate pawn,
even the oceans.
So is the air we breathe,
the lakes and trees.

Objections will be neutralised
as weird, subversive notions.
In profit-led inventiveness,
these systems hover over us
from when we're born
to our assured decease.
It's wearing, on a daily basis,
we recognize, beyond a doubt.
Admitting you've been had's
just one more burden
you can live without.

We clarify your rights
and we appreciate your trust.
We anticipate your protest and
advise against all self-disgust.
So do yourself a favour,
and accept the situation.
Give all the ins and outs of it
their due consideration,
and go easy on yourself,
for rape is rage and tribulation.
Relax and smile; bend over,
learn to love the corporation!

On my life trip I enjoyed motorcycles, many cars, snorkeling, scuba-diving, parachuting, hot-air ballooning, hallucinogenics, and hiking and biking. I've always been a keen swimmer, in pools, lakes and ocean. I've travelled widely; from the Alps, to the Greek Islands to the Florida Keys, the Prairies, the Rocky Mountains, New Zealand, and the countries of S.E. Asia, to name a few of the places I've seen.

Then there were the lovers I've known, the painting I tried, the acting I've done, the four plays I wrote, and saw produced in the London Fringe, the novels I wrote, the Marxist project I advocated, found to be ultimately flawed and murderous, so abandoned. There were the risks I ran, and the accidents I survived, and some lucky escapes.

And all the time there was a poet in me, watching, wondering, rejoicing in his recurrent good luck, waiting to reawaken, hit the release button and emerge. I can't think, honestly, of a comparable life-arc, at any point in human history, to match my generation's trip. That period took in the descent of the Bathysphere, the ascent of the VTOL Harrier jet, and the expansion of Astro-Physics. Big Bang theory replaced Steady State theory. There was the UK's Jodrell Bank pioneering radio telescope, followed by more of them, internationally; the discovery of dark matter, and quasars and pulsars, and black holes and neutrinos and quarks, and the parallel refinement of rocketry and guidance systems. We saw research satellites, the Voyager spacecraft, the construction of the International Space Station, the exploration of our solar system, and the discovery of water on Mars, and the certainty, now, that a Mars settlement will come within decades.

Way back in my life there were born transistors, and the solid state electronics revolution, and the obsolescence of electronic valves. There was anti-noise, anti-matter, carbon-dating, electron-microscopy, micro-processors, micro dots and Nano-technology, new materials and super-conductivity and super-computers. There were still steam trains taking us on holiday when I was a boy. Then came new diesels, then electric trains, then, abroad, bullet trains and under-mountain and undersea railway tunnels, then there was magnetic levitation technology, fusion reactors, national power grids, hydro-electric, wind, and solar power. Oh, and they built the Channel Tunnel, and I've travelled through it by train from London to Paris. I'm merely scratching the surface of a life here.

On my life trip I've seen a huge dumbing–down of society in general, and a decline in educational standards. I'm not imagining that. I worked as a supply teacher in comprehensive schools in England, after I was made redundant in the telecoms industry, and I've interviewed and evaluated numerous candidates for jobs, in various sales-manager roles I had. Neither was an inspiring experience.

The growth of the Internet, and alternative information sources has, on the other hand, severely dented the influence of Establishment mass-media. It has alerted the general public to the destructive consequences of globalization, and the machinations of a corrupt ruling elite, engaged in ushering in a New World Order against their will. It has begun to trigger revolutions, such as the popular resistance, in the UK, to an EU super state, with Brexit, and anti-EU developments elsewhere in Europe. However, the threat of the aggressive advances of militant Islam into democratic and gullible western nations is serious. Free speech, a right valued as paramount through my life, and through the whole western enlightenment, is now under open threat from Political Correctness, and a political "Newspeak" predicted in George Orwell's *1984*. CCTV mass-surveillance, facial-recognition software, and satellite communications have made the Orwellian nightmare of Big Brother a technological reality.

The UK is the most spied-on place on the planet. The society that once gave us Speakers' Corner has morphed into an enemy of free expression, where university students demand "safe spaces" free from the dangerous influence of debate and alternative ideas. Truly bizarre, and possibly, ultimately tragic.

If I were a cynic, I might say I'd seen the best of it.

I'm glad the poet in me stayed the course, and I was hugely amused that, with the amazing launch of AIRSTRIP, at the legendary "Heart of Darkness" club, in Phnom Penh, in December 2017, I made it into a band before I turned seventy! (pause for hoots of self-mockery).

As I go forward, however, there's one abiding influence from my lifetime I can be sure will go along with me, the Uncertainty Principle. As the robotics revolution resurrects the Luddites, and ushers in massive unemployment, that age of plentiful, available jobs I knew in my youth, seems as far-off as James Watt, Brunel, and Hargreaves' Spinning Jenny.

God is dead, but let's hope Artificial Intelligence knows better.

It's not over 'till it's over. Onwards.

Count your blessings.

You grow old, as you have lived,
among charlatans, thieves, political liars,
talentless poseurs, decriers of the worthy,
running on jealousy. And infestations
of academic commissars,
post-modernist frauds.

It's the culture of the cockroaches
and The Murderers of Truth Awards,
the era of the brainwashed and the ordure of
the journo-whores.
Betrayed and dumbed-down i-phone slaves
whose clueless, bovine ignorance
ignores the marxist killing floors,
bloodstained dystopias built on bones.

Whose ignorance of history abjures
the corporate criminals, and Maoist-clones,
the gilded movie bawds, the papal puppeteers and
teflon pederasts, the rackets and
the turnover of temples-become-profit-zones,
the mummery of ritual to stupefy the herd.

In the culture of the cockroaches, subjection
is the meaning, and compliance is the word.
So, count your blessings, poet,
you grow old, as you have lived,
amid the virtue-signalling of herds
of posturing tyros to the left of
the absurd.

KC: How does one improve as a poet – and in what ways have you gotten better at your craft?

JG: With poetry, like most art, given some basic talent, practice is key to improvement, but read other poets, ancient and modern, learn about the tradition and the revolutionaries. Practice at reading aloud is also important, since poetry, it has often been forgotten, is a performance art. This certainly wasn't the emphasis in the teaching I received, but it's an integral part of the bardic and troubadour tradition, literally centuries old. Only recently did I recall my father telling me that he'd often been assigned to give poetic recitations when he was a boy. Apparently he was pretty good at it. As a self-educated man, who missed out on formal schooling, and with an uncaring father forever embittered by the horrors of his soldiering in the First World War, he always encouraged a love of poetry in me. His last words told me to carry on writing it.

Reading aloud builds confidence for the poet, and extends the theatrical dimension of poetic narrative. It does require some acting ability, however; and rehearsal. It's a way to make a poem pack more emotional punch. It's a more direct, if risky, form of communicating the piece. Successful experience in reading aloud also feeds back into the style of writing. For example, it developed the narrative thrust much more in my work.

Also, looking back on it, the weekly pressure to produce a verse column of a comic / satirical nature, to a deadline, was a useful discipline in student days. It taught me more than I realized, in basic technical skills.

Studying for my Master's Degree in Elizabethan and Shakespearian Drama, I had a year of total immersion in the works of Shakespeare and his contemporaries, which had to have a significant formative effect on my own creative development.

After I started writing poetry again, I reached out, about twenty five years ago, to other local poets, in Hertfordshire UK, and started a poets' group which met every week to read and critique members' work. The group, which I believe is still in existence, is called Poetry I.D. (after one of my poems of the same name) and proved very helpful to a number of poets in developing their writing, and gaining confidence in their art. The group organized readings and workshops, and produced an annual poetry collection.

Public readings, with this group, and subsequently, gave me valued experience in delivering and projecting my work. The feedback I received strengthened my self-belief as a poet.

I say, in all seriousness, Poet was a title I was reluctant to adopt lightly. After all my study, my reading, and as a student who had absorbed the ideas of T S Eliot and F R Leavis, the role of poet, to me, was a mantle, sanctified by tradition, something to be earned, rather than claimed. I've seen many people claim it with an embarrassing lack of any skill.

My Facebook page, and the Lizardville Productions Facebook page, have served for some years now, as outlets for my poetry. It has been like being able to give a reading whenever I want to, often several times a week. The positive feedback I've received from a loyal following has been a real stimulus to me as a poet, and I take this opportunity to thank those people for their support. My Poetry Universe page, closed before publication of this book, had gained a thousand "likes."

Though I have had work consistently published, in magazines and websites in the UK and the USA, my adopting the role of "Performance Poet" in S.E. Asia, put the emphasis strongly on live readings. I started live readings at various venues in Bangkok, beginning at a performance evening I started at Assumption University when I was teaching there. I continued in clubs in Bangkok, and still later, Phnom Penh. In the process I got noticed; some called me the "Poet Noir". For me, all this period was one of practice and development in my writing and its delivery.

As my workflow continued, and I was better known, I published two collaborations at Lizardville Productions. *Bangkok, Heart of Noir* was a poetic collaboration with Expressionist painter, Chris Coles. *Blanc et Noir* was a poetic collaboration with photographer, Mark Desmond Hughes.

Working with great talents in other disciplines means you must produce of your best to merit the partnership, I greatly enjoyed complementing my poetry with the impressive output of these two guys.

A final note regarding improving and sustaining one's poetic output, is a simple one. Be attuned and receptive for new ideas, images, inspirations. Always have a notebook with you. Some of those ideas can take months or years to gel.

KC: What has Southeast Asia gotten right that the West never learned? What do you miss about England?

JG: I feel no empathy with the brand of Buddhism in Thailand and Cambodia, even though I've been very influenced and sustained by Zen Buddhism, in my life and thinking.

I've always enjoyed the more tolerant attitudes to some aspects of life, that one found in Thailand. Such open-mindedness seems to be in decline these days, under military dictatorship. However, since Thai tolerance also extends to thoroughgoing social corruption, it's not always a positive thing.

What do I miss about England? Landscapes where I used to go hiking, like The Lake District, Dartmoor, Exmoor, the Yorkshire Dales, and Northumberland.

I miss mountain-biking in a cool climate. I'm also an Irish citizen, and I miss Ireland even more. I go back when I can.

(from) Thoughts from the West

But driving
to the reading up in Donegal,
re-visiting the windy West,
as rapt as any lover,
best redeems a poet,
weaver without witnesses,
invests in me a landscape green
of ancestry and memory.
The straight road to old friendships,
and the boundless zest
of childhood wait within
the healing whisper of the trees.
So, under rolling Sligo skies,
through Drumcliffe, northward,
by Ben Bulben's side, I'm breathless
in the land's embrace,
this stormy blessing of a place
we cried so often, leaving,
lives ago.

KC: You and John Burdett had some major differences over Brexit. I believe you got a nice blurb from John out of it. Explain Brexit. What do the critics not get?

JG: Brexit is about the British people waking up to the fact that their agreement to participate in a European Common Market has been hijacked by a totally different agenda, to become part of a European super state. The following recent press report about recently released government documents, puts it in a nutshell. It describes a political conspiracy against the British public.

   "We were lied to!

   A SECRET document, which remained locked away for 30 years, advised the British Government to COVER-UP the realities of EU membership so that by the time the public realised what was happening it would be too late.

Almost all of the shocking predictions – from the loss of British sovereignty, to monetary union and the over-arching powers of European courts – have come true.

But damningly for Tory Prime Minister Edward Heath, and all those who kept quiet about the findings in the early 70s, the document, known as FCO30/1048, was locked away under Official Secrets Act rules for almost five decades.

The classified paper, dated April 1971, suggested the Government should keep the British public in the dark about what EEC membership means, predicting that it would take 30 years for voters to realise what was happening, by which time it would be too late to leave.

That last detail was the only thing the disgraceful paper – prepared for the Foreign and Commonwealth Office (FCO) – got wrong.

This 1971 document shows exactly what the plan was.

The unknown author – a senior civil servant – correctly predicted the then European Economic Community (the EEC effectively became the EU in 1993) was headed for economic, monetary and fiscal union, with a common foreign and defence policy, which would constitute the greatest surrender of Britain's national sovereignty since 1066.

He went on to say "Community law" would take precedence over our own courts , and that ever more power would pass away from Parliament to the bureaucratic system centred in Brussels.

The author even accurately asserts that the increased role of Brussels in the lives of the British people would lead to a "popular feeling of alienation from Government".

But, shockingly, politicians were advised "not to exacerbate public concern by attributing unpopular measures… to the remote and unmanageable workings of the Community". "

After David Cameron, the former Prime Minister, through a combination of arrogance and incompetence, stumbled into offering a referendum on Britain's membership of the EU, the Establishment's absurdly exaggerated warnings against leaving (now derided as "The Big Fear") became comic legend. Increased unemployment was the least there was to fear, according to this huge propaganda campaign. From the lock-stepped apparatchiks of the BBC to pop-music has-beens like Bob Geldoff, to political-has beens like John Major, to soon-to- be's like Hillary Clinton and Barrack Obama, there were dire warnings of disaster, toil and trouble, if their beloved New World Order was disrupted. The UK Chancellor, Osborne made predictions of such spookily dire outcomes that the biblical plagues of Egypt seemed preferable to leaving the EU. This arch- black-propagandist, whose fictitious predictions patronized and insulted the public's intelligence, was fired from the cabinet after the vote to leave. However, he has since been appointed the Editor of London's mass circulation daily paper, The Evening Standard. As my American friends would say, "Go figure!"

And the cost has been huge.

In addition to this eye-watering slice of taxpayers' money, the government also gave away the UK's right to make its own laws and determine its own tax rates, gave away its rich fisheries, and surrendered a thousand years of English Common Law to the European Court.

Unregulated immigration of unskilled workers drove working class wages down, swamped the National Health Service, and flooded schools with non-English speakers.

About 1.95 million European nationals have moved to Britain since Poland and nine former Soviet bloc countries joined the EU in 2004, giving them freedom to come and work in the UK.

This compares to 1.49m migrants from countries outside the EU settling in Britain in the same time.

This means Britain's population has increased by about six percent, due solely to non-British immigrants, in a decade.

People who drew attention to these alarming figures were smeared as racists, extremists, nationalist, and right-wingers, in a full-on BBC and mass-media onslaught, reminiscent, in its ruthless thoroughness, of the work of Joseph Goebbels, and presaging the totally manipulated and discredited mass media we endure today.

However, as we saw, the British public were not fooled. They voted to leave the EU, because they had real personal experience of a drastic fall in the quality of life for ordinary folk, which fat-cat supporters of the EU membership did not.

Since that fateful vote to leave, we've seen the full weight of the UK establishment, from the BBC to the Lords, and ranks of rich media airheads, and patronizing EU hirelings, employed in an anti-democratic effort to deride, thwart, and possibly reverse the decision of seventeen and a half million Britons, to leave the EU.

Their masters, in Berlin and Brussels, urge them on, clearly alarmed at the imminent loss of the UK economy and its riches, from their super-state game-plan.

That, in brief, is the reality of Brexit. Escape from a masterpiece of lies.

KC: Can you separate your life from your poetry? How are they separate? How are they intertwined?

JG: They are inseparable. Writing a poem that works well is one of life's high-order pleasures. It is completely habit-forming.

PROCESSING

Of all the landmarks of the Forbidden City
which embellish this ruined quarter,
the Tower of Yearning still crackles
with lonely life.
Stored hereabouts is Dowland's Lachrimae
and other melancholy data.
Here, gloomy church interiors,
journals of half-forgotten wars
and maps of vanished cities crowd
the great soliloquies.
There, a Roman amphitheatre
vibrating to the late quartets,
a pocketful of lunar rubble,
huge with silence, older than God.

For ages, keeping this from crumbling
into other data, bleeding into becoming,
I've tried sealing off the entire sector.

But it leaks remembrance, unconsoled;
like old reactor rivets,
hot for another quarter million years.

"Ordo Ab Chao" is the Latin expression that defines why writing poetry
is addictive. It means Order out of Chaos. Poetry is a rich discipline that
allows you to visit life events that might otherwise be overwhelming,
scary, inspiring; as a poet, to come back with something to say, to
process them, into art. Poetry always did that.

If you get to the stage of delivering your poetry in public, and you are
successful, you additionally get the actor's or musician's performance
feedback. So, yes, poetry, among other things, is life therapy. It's also a
craft, of course, so without that skill component, and practice, it will be
bad poetry.

It's pretty scary thinking about drying up.

Creative cold turkey would be a serious hurdle to manage.

Here is the Muse

And when she saves your lucky skin again,
incredibly she opens to your tentative embraces,
and has you, in the hallway of the treasury,
some happy fool, exalted to be chosen, momentarily;
allowed to see her naked faces,
intimate, contemptuous, by turns.

She's left you in the empty morning,
grateful, and alone again,
her number smeared like lipstick in your notebook,
and seems a fragrant phantom then,
till evidenced by carpet burns.

Short of a Beethoven string quartet, few art forms have the emotional depth, eloquence, and richness of poetry at its best. An awareness of a place in the long literary tradition enriches a writer and supplies a kind of empowering alchemy. Isaac Newton famously wrote in 1675: "If I have seen further it is by standing on the shoulders of Giants."

That's exactly the way "The Great Tradition" can elevate and empower you, as a writer, if you can also bring something special of your own to the party.

TRUE DETECTIVE.

On the client's balcony,
an answer hit me, vertigo high,
"One bad attitude's
enough to find damnation."
Sure; that's why I slid through
those realities that evening
on his tuner, found this
case had grown impossibly big.
Heard the laughter from inside....

"Was just radio noise", he testified,
"until I stumbled on the integrator switch,
and the whole gig went harmonic."
Subversive hospitality; party-lover.
Said he's seen too much now,
can't go back there.
Batshit crazy;
or may just be a Buddha.

Altered and illegal states cheat
fiction, I told my client, later.
Naked laughter from the room behind.

"We're locked into this caper,
brother. We score by bringing
something special to the party;
one way, or another".

Time to go back, inside.

**KC: The legacy of many a great poet includes the fact there is little to
no money derived from the art. How would John Gartland like to be
remembered? What do you hope readers of your poems, including the
ones in this book, will learn from their reading in the year 2068?**

JG: Remembered for and by the work only. Oblivion is much more
likely.

Oblivion to Bang Wa.

I'm looking, for the thousandth time,
down from this commuter line
at a weedy Chinese graveyard,
sliding by.
It says memory's a shaky act.

Oblivion Junction to Bang Wa.
The rush-hour train is packed,
approaching Saleh Daeng;
our Skytrain, slowing down
now, for the station.

And over crumbling vaults,
the ring of corporate giants
looms in stainless expectation
of a drop-dead valuation,
for this real-estate of tombs.

And suddenly, statistically,
you know that someone
on this train, will get off
at big Junction O, today;
will never have another
job to sweat about, or have
another monthly pass to pay.

And in another hundred years, or less,
say seventy five, not one aboard
Oblivion to Bang Wa now will be alive,
and many here today can't know,
that they're already booked to go,
express.

No one stayed top-dog, fatcat,
mad-ass, high-so, in-crowd.
No one stayed hot, stayed high,
stayed strong, stayed up-and-coming,
loaded, or knew why they didn't give
a fuck for any of it, anymore.
Of course, long dead, or ga-ga,
they're guaranteed not to.

But some are heard laughing,
Oblivion to Bang Wa,
some are still laughing
in books that they left you.

KC: Talk about humility. What does it mean to you, if anything.

JG: As the Ancient Greek writers knew well, hubris invites nemesis.
    In the face of the abiding mysteries of life and death, the philosopher
knows humility is the wisest virtue.

Witness Statement

Lost beauty, and lost self-respect, lost scope.
Lost joy, lost peace, lost self-belief, lost hope...
And owning
the pathology of moral dissolution
is revolving-door to wisdom
(when self-knowledge realigns us).
There's no impartial witness statement
here, in life's bargain self-a-basement.
It is our naked suffering defines us.

In the time of slippage,
insincerity and drift,
he'd lived in many places,
gathering up the thoughts of man,
embracing the forbidden,
and concealed behind an actor's faces.
A Jungian meditation saved him.
Analysis the fix began...

"Lost love and lost compassion and lost pages.
Lost chances, and lost promise and lost ages.
I squandered all my assets and rejected every boss.
Though often high, and sometimes drunk,
I know I was a pilgrim monk
for Fragments of the True Loss.
I write a witness statement
from the pit of Purgatory, brother.
I write a hack of self-discovery,
a true confession, and no other.
Lost passion, and lost confidence, lost heart.
Lost pity, lost integrity, lost freedom, and lost art.

Each humbling profanity,
each annihilating breath
are assassins to our vanity,
and naked dress-rehearsals
for the opening-night of death.

I owned self-hatred as my name,
the peace of understanding was the prize.
No glitz or lies can mar my game,
no cataclysm, wound or dross.
Redeemed the world with different eyes,
I guard the Fragments of True Loss."

No fix, no hold, no grip
and no abiding plan,
the slide into the
mystery of True Loss
distinguishes, then
levels every man.

Photograph by Eric Nelson

CHAPTER 11

Book Review of Vincent Calvino's World
by Chad Evans

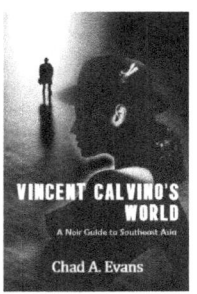

"With the knowledge gained it becomes difficult to imagine the political upheavals, the social and technological change and the noir corruption enveloping the characters of the street in modern Southeast Asia without Vincent Calvino. He is our street guide through the noir side of the Bangkok night, our cultural interpreter of fast-changing Thai and expat society on all levels, our go-between leading us through fictional situations which are synchronous with real time recent history. And he is a devil for the detail of Thai behavior, language, belief systems and the inner workings of the powerful." *Vincent Calvino's World* by Chad Evans.

Certain books come around where the idea had crossed my mind previously. *Vincent Calvino's World* by Chad Evans is one such book. I can remember thinking, fleetingly, as a fan of the series there should be a book that chronicles the now 15 strong Vincent Calvino novels written by the Canadian author, Christopher G. Moore. The thought was fleeting because I had to consider who would be crazy enough to take on such a daunting, challenging task and give it the merit and due diligence it deserved? Not me, I was sure of that. Chad A. Evans is, evidently, crazy enough and talented enough to get the job done well. And thank the gods or the animals (up to you) for that.

This book, which encapsulates the essence and nuance of a fictional character, a gifted and principled author, the time and place of a region, and a culture is now on the shelves or a digital world near you. Like the Vincent Calvino crime novels, Moore's stand-alone fiction, and his four books of essays they are all available at this moment in time and for future generations.

William Faulkner in a 1956 Paris Review interview said, "The aim of every artist is to arrest motion, which is life, by artificial means and hold it fixed so that a hundred years later, when a stranger looks at it, it moves again, since it is life."

Both the author Chad Evans and the creator of the fictional private detective Vincent Calvino have taken life and characters and arrested motion taking place over three decades in multiple ways. For the fan of the Vincent Calvino series, and they exist around the globe, the purchase of this book is an easy call to make. For anyone interested in the culture and politics of Thailand and the region it is a book to be enjoyed, to be appreciated and to be savored. Evans deciphers how Moore has been able to both entertain and educate the reader on topics of law, culture, romance, transactional sex, violence, corruption, technology and history. If you have read one Vincent Calvino novel or all fifteen, you will enjoy this excellent case study. If not, read *Vincent Calvino's World* first, it will make you want to do so. In that same Paris Review interview Faulkner goes on to say,

"Since man is mortal, the only immortality possible for him is to leave something behind him that is immortal since it will always move. This is the artist's way of scribbling "Kilroy was here" on the wall of the final and irrevocable oblivion through which he must someday pass."

If Faulkner is right; the immortality of Christopher G. Moore is assured. No study of Moore's books would be complete without referring to a piece of Chad Evans' own legacy, *Vincent Calvino's World*. What a treat it is to read. What a tribute it carves for Moore, today, and for eternity. Moore maintains that only a sliver of history is recorded, a splinter if you will. The rest is forgotten all too soon. The world is a better place for the sliver of moments Moore has documented and Evans has reviewed. Both writers leave the reader knowing what a splendid splinter it is. *Vincent Calvino's World* is equally entertaining and educational, a perfect pitch noir guide to Southeast Asia. Well done, Chad A. Evans.

Author Chad Evans

CHAPTER 12

An Interview with Chad Evans

KC: You've got another book out, *Vincent Calvino's World*, a book I very much enjoyed reading. What was the motivation to take on such a project – what compelled you, besides sure-fire fame, riches and glory?

CE: I have never had any motivation other than envy, and desire to catch up with my gifted son, in some small measure (he remarked, wickedly) since he occupies such an eminent position now, in SE Asian archaeology and anthropology. So Dad had to do something.

Basically I glanced at a *Thai Lonely Planet* guidebook after having a good time in that country for a few weeks, and saw a mention of a crime novelist, C.G. Moore. So I found two of his titles in Oz in the lending system: *Spirit House* and *Risk of Infidelity Index* and read them. I have probably read 7 or 8 thousand crime novels. But I was so impressed. It was like I was reading my own writing, like I was reading a successful creative version of myself. So I tossed an email at this author, Christopher G. Moore, saying this, and not only did he reply, he said he felt as though I had given him the ultimate praise from the heart.

KC: Who were some of your earliest influences in crime fiction and literature? Please be sure and include at least one Australian author.

CE: Garry Disher is my main crime guy in Oz. I mean he writes procedurals and criminal POV novels . . . furthermore what I respect about him most is he wrote the best book ever on how to write a novel. So a teacher, and not just a writer. Carol O'Connell is a class act as far as I am concerned, her Mallory novels have that wonderful accessibility for men ... Despite a superwoman feminist aspect, the heroine is an absolute sociopath. James Lee Burke for his Faulkner hypnotic-poetic prose, but my main influences personally as a writer are mid-20th Century guys, possibly the same as Christopher's actually ... I liked Steiner and Koestler; both polymaths, fully evolved left and right side brain guys. Plus they had Euro angst. I was most influenced in my formative years by a clutch of Canadian writers. I was mentored by a Wiccan poet, Robin Skelton ... so was Margaret Atwood, so I was in good company there. Robin and Ferlinghetti were good West Coast mates, so I was just a youngling at the haunted house parties Robin used to hold in his Queen Anne style house, one night each week. It was a house filled with artists, booze and, you name it. Then Robertson Davies impacted on me in a big way (he was my Master at Massey College, University of Toronto). It was like confronting the most famous novelist in the world for a few years there. He taught me that a 63 year old could come off the practice course and go 10 under par in the U.S. Open. Aside from that I would say playscripts were my biggest influence. I read them all, from Aeschylus to Pinter, and, really I hate to tell you this ... dramatists are light years ahead of most novelists, as artists who understand the human condition. Fiction is about wasting time mostly. Not so, plays.

KC: Tell our readers about your previous writing projects. Did they prepare you for writing *Vincent Calvino's World*?

There was a sea-witch, Susan Musgrave I think, who my Grade 10 teacher and other boffins were acknowledging as the great writerly hope. I was in the same class. Anyway I won the short story competition with a pornographic cookery recipe story ... light years before this became a TV idiom.

I guess you might say I was extremely well-educated in the late 1960s and early 70s. I was a Canadian West Coaster, and locally we got the cream of American talent smart enough to escape the Vietnam Draft. Very radical guys all of them. This was my classroom, packing an anti-nuke banner past John Wayne's converted minesweeper, and him on the prow waving his finger at the slope-shouldered Canuck kid: "Don't tell us what to do with our bombs, son."

Then this this western cowboy went to Massey College, University of Toronto, and got the top grade of world thinkers: George Steiner, Frye, McLuhan, Ann Saddlemyer, et al . . . an embarrassment of intellectual riches, really, at that time. Funny thing is, we all ate the same meal every night at this underground place on Bloor Street, one dish, Hungarian Goulash plus a loaf, nothing else, and here you had Gordon Lightfoot, Josef Skvorecky, Maggie Atwood, McLuhan, Ondaatje, endless genius communicators and uni. students all stuffing themselves with this goulash. I still dream about that joint. The communist meal was better than you think. Food so simple you had to talk about other matters.

Anyway, back to soporific Vancouver Island after that, oh about 1975, and half the population of the island seem to be relatives of mine, and I wrote a novel, then was drafted into the new heritage conservation bureaucratic movement as a thinker. The first thinking involved discovering in my attic the complete architectural drawings for the beautiful Parliament Buildings and Empress Hotel in Victoria, British Columbia.

So as a civil servant on contract I began to research and write about the 'entertainment' history of the Far West, and that grew into my book *Frontier Theatre* which hit the U.S. shelves in 1984. I was like a rogue academic . . . too dangerous to actually employ within universities (5 have made attempts) a kind of lost intellectual soul until Christopher G. Moore pried the lid off me.

KC: What do you hope the reader takes away from reading *Vincent Calvino's World*? Why should it be read?

CE: Surely the underlying message is Southeast Asia is, or has been, the most interesting place on earth, because it allowed us a kind of time travel for a spell. Sadly, the Chinese overlords are now building dams and tyrannical spheres of influence along the Mekong. It is the saddest story on the planet. Real people are being displaced by dictators and Red corporatism. I mourn the wild creatures in the Cambodian forests.

I am old school, like a Moog synthesizer, and I suppose I was influenced by George Steiner and Arthur Koestler more than other writers. You know, a polymath-type, bridging everything, pooling all the connections, meaning I wanted my book *Vincent Calvino's World* to be the one-stop cultural museum for SE Asia. It is not as easy as it looks . . . creating a monograph that will stand through time as a necessary reference. It probably helped that I have Khmer family, and we're very close, so the emotional bond was pre-formed before I executed a major intellectual examination of the region and culture using Christopher G. Moore's fiction as my prism. I thought this Moore guy deserved, for so many reasons, to be treated like the great writer he is. Like a Thai dish, my offering has the full spectrum of color and taste, and any serious reader should enjoy the meal if they sustain an open mind. Thailand and Cambodia are places that change you forever.

KC: Early on in *VCW* you describe Calvino as a closet humanist. For readers who may be unaware of Vincent Calvino, describe who he is and elaborate on some of his humanist qualities, and explain why it's a good idea he remain in the closet. Or should he now come out?

CE: Ha! First up, thanks for the breezy little question, Kevin.

Look, whether you are a detective or a dangerous writer, you pretty much have the same situation. If you reach say, the age of 45, you will have learned the drill, the margins of discovery, creativity and truth. You know you live in a veil of lies and must be a submariner: run silent run deep like Calvino does.

I am not sure if America, or Canada for that matter, produces Vincent Calvino's anymore, existential beings who are honest, and straight up, and do not subscribe to all the media porridge. Calvino, via his accidental approaches to truth, finds the truth in the end and discovers that the world does not want his discovery. Our world is a world of lies, not truth. Otherwise how else could we mammals destroy most of the planet, and the capitalist vermin talk about bigger suburbs and more population? If that is not dementedly sick, what is?

Sometimes it is all about space. I used to box a bit, and I learned, like a stage ballerina, my map, the perimeter, the length of my left jab, down to the millimeter. I could always feel that rope near my ass. Maintaining proper distance is all, and Calvino, through his creator, sustains a kind of calculated distance, which is disrupted by his uninvited noir involvements. So maybe the big story is how did this guy survive in such a dangerous neighborhood for, oh thirty years.

I am biased. C.G. Moore and I come from very similar backgrounds (something I did not know, incidentally when I took on the impossible job of writing a biography of a fictional character created by a living author living in a foreign country). By similar I mean we come from a time when people still loved, and stood up for, and finished the damn job, without this chorus of media whining about being abused, or oppressed, that we have, ad nauseam, now. Just get the job done and shut up.

But to answer your question, Kevin, well Vinny is maybe the kind of boomer hard-core guy my generation all wanted to be: tough yet sophisticated, a boxer who speaks heart talk. If you want life you have to reach out . . . people in trouble reach out to Calvino . . . and he does not flinch. Even more so, he is utterly independent, and really if you look behind the plots . . . he picks his own cases by inventing them.

KC: In a recent Bangkok Post there is a piece by Stephen L. Carter where he quotes Blakey Vermeule, an English professor at Stanford University, author of *Why Do We Care About Literary Characters*: "Fiction rather uniquely primes our moral intuitions, our sense of right and wrong, of good and bad, of fair and not fair. When we suspect that justice is being thwarted, we want to lodge a protest--and the protest is a deeply moral one, against the unfairness of outcomes." Does Calvino prime a reader's moral intuition?

CE: Ha! Another very complex question. Well ......

To some extent Calvino is a serial mistake artist. His main flaw, the one some of us really love (easier to do with a fictional than a real person) is he does not learn to stop repeating his prime moral mistake. He does not just leave the body alone. His morality is the repetitive weakness we Westerners love to share, Sisyphus stuff really. But no, Calvino has nothing to do with simple fiction equations of right and wrong, good and bad, black or white. His noir is a noir of futile responsibility, as he is incapable of just zoning out into a kind of Zen cloud of dissociation from earthly troubles. Most individuals with Eastern wisdom just shake their head and think: why does this guy not just step off and avoid the troubles? It goes to his demons. There is always a bad guy in the ring. This bad force is the noir you cannot escape.

CHAPTER 13

An Interview with Hugh Gallagher
AKA Von Von Von

KC: Who is Hugh Gallagher, where do you come from and what makes Bangkok, Thailand the base camp of choice for you?

HG: Genetically I have risen from the soils of Ireland. My grandparents came to the US, landed in New York, and that's where I started. Then I grew up in the Philadelphia suburbs, returned to New York to attend NYU and lived in NYC for most of my life. I've also lived 5 years in Portland, Oregon, and 4 in Bangkok. Although an idol of mine would say "it ain't where you're from, it's where you at."

Bangkok surprised me when I landed here. I had no preconception of the city, and I was just amazed at how vibrant, funky, and alive it is. I loved that it had almost no artistic or literary tradition, unlike the West. There are tons of writers who have done Paris, or Mexico, or Italy, or even Japan, Jamaica. Lots of foreign lands fly flags on the expat literary map. Bangkok was just not on that map, as far as I had seen. So it felt like discovery. And it wasn't like I always dreamed of coming here. So I hit the ground very open minded, expecting very little. What I found is what lots of people love about this town. It's both fast and relaxed, fascinating and opaque, smoky and bright. Epic party town. Dripping with sex. I met a great bunch of expats through comedy nights and jazz jams, and made Thai friends playing badminton. Add cheap rents and cheap food—which every creative person needs— and you have a wonderful place to work. Plus you have these beaches, very easy to access through trains and there's cheap hotels everywhere. Love it.

KC: Among your many accomplishments you appeared center stage, alone, at the Apollo Theater in Harlem, New York, and completely won over the audience. That has to rank right up there with playing Carnegie Hall. Tell me about that entire episode. What led up to getting that gig? What happened of note during the performance?

HG: Before Von Von Von, I had a writing career which included features for Rolling Stone and Wired, and a novel published by Simon and Schuster. But the planes hit the World Trade Center and it really changed everything. The mood was so dark, so depressing, so wounded. The last place you wanted to be was sitting in your room all day alone, tripping on it. Which is what writers do. I just had to be out there, I had to be with people. Others must have felt the same as I did because there was this whole underground neo-vaudeville performance art thing happening, mostly based in Brooklyn. I put together Von Von Von. I was living on Tenth Avenue, across from the projects, but right around the corner from all these high powered art galleries. I went to openings because they had free wine and lots of my friends were visual artists. I think that mix of rich, European collectors, and street culture found its form in vVv. So I wrote some songs, found a *faux* fur coat went out there. I first performed in some art galleries and bars and then had a weekly show at this place called Galapagos.

It was really fun, but really enormously challenging. I was always hungry. I had no money. I was trying to figure out how to get over in the music industry, which is just the most brutal beast out there. Musicians are the toughest people in the world. Writers have to be strong. Musicians have to be tough. Warriors. There's so much darkness in the business, metaphorically and also literally, as much of the cash changes hands after hours, when the show is over, and there's liquor bottles all over the place in the club. Fucked. Crazy.

Hugh Gallagher as Von Von Von

Anyway, I'm trying to find my way through this low rent, after hours, downtown maze when I heard this ad on the radio one day. I was just lying in my apartment and this voice came on saying "Would YOU like to be on the world famous APOLLO THEATRE?! Come audition for Showtime!" I jumped up, got a pen, and wrote down the address for the audition spot. It was a community center somewhere up on like 144th Street. Line around the block. People had flown in from North Carolina, Florida. Heads from all over New York. It was like a pilgrimage for black performers and entertainers. It's such a hallowed hall. I waited in line for about four hours, did my thing, and they sent me a letter in the mail a few weeks later. It was red. Had the Apollo letter head in big red spot-lights. I spent my last money on a good haircut, went up to the Apollo and hit it.

The funny thing about that performance—and what was cut from the show—was that I was booed off the stage TWICE before I even opened my mouth. I walked out there, chalk white, in a fur vest and Harlem Just. Wasn't. Having. That. Not at all. Finally, the host Rudy Rush calmed them down. I remember him saying—"C'mon Harlem,

give this brother a chance, he flew all the way from Antwerp." Then I went out there and it was all love. Puts a smile on my face just thinking about it. One of the best experiences of my life, hands down. And stakes were high. Back then they still had the Sandman. He would come out wearing diapers, dancing, and shoot you with a toy bow and arrow if you got booed off. You didn't want that happening to you. It didn't. I just totally got over. The band rocked, I hit my mark and we lit up Harlem. Felt like walking on the moon. Blessed.

KC: Ever since Kato Kaelin came along, fame has been devalued in the USA. Unlike Kato, you are multi-talented, a traditionally published novelist, comedian, musician, writer, and even have your own apartment. You've captured fame and notoriety. You've held it and tasted it. More than once. You talk about the fame game at HughGallagher.net and how difficult the rules of engagement are. Tell me about the pursuit of fame, the achievements you are most proud of, and the difficulties that come with taking fame to the household name level.

HG: I feel that finding fame is accidental. You do something, it hits, and Fame on. Once you have it, there are things you can do to build and reinforce it. I do what interests me and what I love. Because most projects have a really long build. Books take years, so did Von Von Von. You have to stay with it. It takes so much will power and belief and love for what you're doing that for me, there's no way I could just do something to be famous. That being said- and tying into your thoughts about the devaluation of fame—we're in a culture where Fame=Success. If you don't catch fame, you drown and die. Nobody sees you. Nobody talks about you. So whatever you do, you have to make it famous to really get over. That's not a science I've perfected. I've done lots of things that haven't hit at all. The funny thing is that my college essay is more famous than I am. It's all over the place. It was the first viral comedy hit of the internet, and it's one of the most famous pieces of written American humor. I'm amazed at how many people have read it. But not so many people know I wrote it. So it goes.

The great thing about fame is that people want to meet you, and work comes to you. Most of our life—everybody—we're hustling. We're trying to get jobs, trying to get paid, trying really hard to fight our way up the slanted landscape. When you're famous, the landscape tilts towards you. Opportunities, jobs, and women come to you. You don't have to chase. You get a team around you that handles and manages your business, and that's great if you have the right people. That part of business gets easier, and it's a tremendous relief, and a huge advantage that lets you work without stressing the rent. With a steady stream of offers and opportunities, life is great.

But it does bring other stressors. People expect you to rock every spot the way your big hits have. There's less room to make mistakes. Fame moves fast, and you have to roll with it or lose it. I think that's why lots of popular artists get in a loop with their work. What made them famous is encouraged by their team and their fans. It's very hard to break off into new territory. And breaking into new territory is a sloppy process. You make mistakes finding your way. Famous people aren't really supposed to make mistakes. If they do, a lot of shit comes down on them, and they lose lots of fans, maybe even their fame.

After I did the Apollo, I had Harlem fame, which was probably the coolest shit ever. I was recording up on 155th street, so I was always up around Jackie Robinson Park, or on the A train uptown. So many people would pass me on the street and be like: "Yo Von." Just that. Or "Hey Von." Real low key and familiar, maybe a fist bump and that's all. You're walking down 125 and some real big black dude passes by with a "Alright von", little head nod, it just rocks. I remember one night very late on the train, I was exhausted, had been recording, it was four in the morning probably, and I always wore my shades in the train at night because the lights are so bright and the ride is long. So I'm half falling asleep, and half wondering what the hell I'm doing with my life. I mean, there I am in a fur coat on a train from Harlem at 4 a.m. in the middle of a pretty absurd recording career. Where is this all going? What the hell am I doing? Then I heard laughter across the train. It got louder, and these kids were just busting up. Three fifteen year old black kids, with the NYC flat brim hats, the tims, big old jeans, everything. And they were just lit up laughing, and I heard one of them say "That's Von Von Von."

KC: Pablo Picasso said, "Inspiration exists, but it has to find you working." What inspires you? Tell me about some of your work.

HG: Great quote. I'm one of those shark writers. You know how sharks die if they stop swimming? I can't handle reality without writing. I'm wired for it. I have to do it. Whether people are reading or not, it just balances me out. If I stop I get really edgy and unsettled. Not that I'm a lake of tranquility when I'm living as a writer. But I feel in tune. Writing just flows through me. I do the best I can to manage it.

Inspiration to write comes from different places. The inspiration for *Teeth* came from spending lots of time within the US pop culture machine. It's this thing that pumps out so much flash but very little introspection. I wanted to trip on it for a while, and explore the reality beyond the façade. My college essay started because I was bored in a high school typing class. They had all this boring shit we were supposed to type and I just started writing all this wild stuff to entertain myself and crack up my friends. At the same time, I was applying for colleges, so the two things merged and found form.

Von Von Von was all about being out there, my love of music, having fun, and creating an idealized life style that I wanted, but was out of reach. I couldn't fly around the world and make love, but I could sing about it.

Lifted, my lizard people sci-fi book, was inspired after Von Von Von failed. I had failed, 100% for the first time in my life. I had to process it. I dipped into lots of ancient spiritual texts, and realized that very few of them say planet earth is a good place. And I had met a dude talking about lizard people at a Los Angeles UFO convention I wrote about in the nineties. After all the failure I had been through, and all the freaky weird shit I had seen in the music industry, it wasn't hard to believe this world is run by monsters. Before I had a lot of success and life was fun. I mean, it was still Life, it's hard, but I was getting paid and getting invited to great parties. When all that fell off I saw life from another angle. I had to find hope for myself, and inspiration, that was entirely free from worldly success or acceptance by the larger culture. These great characters started coming to me, and the lizard people is such a funky funny idea that I rolled with it. The writing process was exhilarating. The characters were very alive for me. They got me through that time in my life by giving me a story to help understand loss, disappointment, and the harder parts of life. Then I could say: fuck it, I'm still fighting. Maybe that's all that book was for. Just helping me get through losing everything and starting from scratch.

The ghostwriting book and the doomed time travel thriller were both inspiring because they paid. Then I got into it and it was a blast writing trashy thrillers. Sex scenes, meetings at the Pentagon, shit blowing up... So ridiculous and so fun to write.

Yo Ching was inspired by True Player. What he said, and the wisdom he had was so deep for me. It's a treasure of life strategy. There's so much in that book about how to flow with reality. And I love the way he phrases things. It's the only cosmic, timeless truth filled book that uses the word "motherfucker." Plus I have this huge love of hip hop culture, and uptown NYC culture. I lived way up in Harlem for years, then deep in the Bronx. I was an outsider but I heard stuff, I saw stuff- it's like this whole other world, as deep as any foreign country. An essential element of black culture that inspires me most is the "show and prove" thing. "You were great yesterday, fine. Show me. Prove it. Right here, right now." Or: "Oh, you're doing what you did yesterday and you still think that shit is great today? Next." No one gets a pass. It shapes their artists into fiercely innovative creators. As a 14 year old kid learning drums, I was listening to drummers like Elvin Jones and Tony Williams, trying to understand how they played with time. Shit they do is wildly sophisticated. As an 18 year old trying to find my voice as a writer, I was having my mind blown by hip hop artists like Rakim and Chuck D. Those men put words together like tapestries. Some of their rhymes should be framed in the Smithsonian. I have gotten so much from their culture that I wanted to celebrate it. True Player, who's from the Bronx, gave me that chance when I met him. I was also trying to find a way to share the blessing of living in Asia with friends from home. I wanted to bring some of this part of the world to them. Which is a whole other planet. So I guess I went to two different planets and wanted to write it down.

How all this happens is random. I don't have a defined method, theory or path. Things hit me. If they hit me hard enough, I run with them.

KC: Let's talk books. Around the time your first novel, *Teeth* was published Amazon lost almost $700,000,000 in one year, the Kindle did not exist and previous E-readers had flopped. Fast forward fifteen years and you come out with, *Yo Ching: Ancient Knowledge for Streets Today*, which you produced in collaboration with True Player, a wise man of the streets. Tell me about the two books. Comment on the tsunami of change that has occurred during your professional writing career.

HG: My writing career started on a very traditional literary path. I was published in Harpers as a young one, did features for Rolling Stone as a teenager, then wrote for Wired, and a few other smaller magazines, and then landed a book deal with Simon and Schuster. They really invested in me. Put me on tour, bought out ad pages, and really put money into the goal of launching me. A first time writer could not hope for more. But the sales didn't follow. This happens often in publishing, where books and authors can take time to find their audience. Unfortunately, I didn't have money to wait that out. I had to find work. So I turned down a chance to write another book, because after the taxes, agency fee, and just the time it takes to write, I would have had to leave NYC, which I didn't want to do at the time. *Teeth* disappeared and I fell out of the literary world.

Through a man to whom I will always be grateful —huge shout out to Jonathan Cohen of Critical Mass in NYC—I got into advertising. The release of *Teeth* had been disappointing, and I was bitching about it while we walked through Central Park on a beautiful sunny day.

Jonathon listened about as long as he could. Then he was like "Dude, I hate to break it to you, but having your first book be a best seller is about as likely as us getting struck by lightning right now. If you want to make a living, look into branding and advertising. I can help you." He did. He knew some people at Arnell, and I met Sara Arnell and started learning branding. Arnell Group was like the inventor of the stuff, led by this DaVinci type visionary Peter Arnell who had helped launch Tommy Hilfiger. There was so much interesting shit flying through that office— designers, architects, writers, installation artists. This was late nineties. Digital culture was just starting. They were really hammering out the future of branding in the digital age. And they paid their people well. Which was great. Everything I learned there and throughout a 15+ year career in branding and advertising that followed came into play when I finally published my next book, *YO CHING*.

The source material of *YO CHING* was hugely inspiring on its own: an interactive, decision-making tool based on the oldest book on the planet... China's *I Ching*. The wisdom from this book has been around for 3,000 years. Things survive that long for a reason. They work. *YO CHING* has so much wisdom to help people live better. It's real. It's not one of these "dream it, you can do it!" life strategy books. Those books sell not because they are true, but because everybody wants to be told they can be anything and have it all. They can't. We live in reality. It has rules. Go dream of being a multi-millionaire pantomime artist. See what happens. You have to recognize what's working in reality, and how to flow with it. That might seem basic, but people are moving farther and farther from reality every day. We live in bubbles of entertainment and prepared experiences. We stare at screens and think that's life. It's not. Look out the window. That's life. True Player, the visionary genius behind *YO CHING*, would reflect on this shit in very entertaining ways. He is deep, funny, and very inspiring.

With my first book, *Teeth* it had been about me, my feelings, and was based on my life. Many years later, I had been around the block a few times and "escaped the tyranny of self" as Gore Vidal has so eloquently described the process of growing as a writer. What he means—I think— is that you have to get over yourself. Forget your limited view and see the larger picture. *YO CHING* is definitely about the larger picture. True Player, my collaborator, looks at nature, the galaxy, he references the ocean, the cycle of a star's life, and then relates that to how society moves, how people interact, how business is done, how eras rise and fall. Shit like that is large. I was into it. I loved it. I was ready for it. What I love about *Teeth* is it helped me figure myself out. *YO CHING* helped me figure the world out. And I thought *YO CHING* would be helpful to others too. It's ethically and morally strong, without being sanctimonious. It combines an open spirituality with pragmatic realism. The lessons inside provide strategies for managing reality at optimum levels. It's not a "me" book—it's a "we" book that shows how to harmonize with others, so everybody improves together.

KC: Managing reality. That sounds useful. Hugh, this interview is running long, but I like The Paris Review interviews. Tell me more.

HG: If *YO CHING* started with the words "this is what you have to do" your mind would instantly throw up defenses that are hard to get through—nobody likes to be told what to do. But how can you be defensive against six lines of illustration? Or some abstract poetic statement? You can't—and in fact, the opposite happens. Your mind opens up, searching for reasons, explanations, and the defenses are down. After that, YO slips in the Knowledge. This is highly sophisticated shit. And this structure goes back 3000 years. The most modern arts of Neuro Linguistic Programming use similar tactics. NLP Jedi warriors will do shit like lead with statements that make no sense, or have no real meaning. The most famous being "once upon a time" to start stories. I mean, what does that mean? Why does it start every story? For no reason than disarming the listener, and letting the storyteller past the subconscious defensive systems we all have.

That's why I love *YO CHING*—there are so many levels to what's happening in that book.

The language is plain and blunt, sometimes humorous, deceptively casual. But there are tremendous depths of knowledge within. The more a reader meditates on *YO CHING*, Staying Chill with the learning, the more they will uncover.

CHAPTER 14

Long Live King Klashorst ...
Long Live The King

Peter Klashorst in his Phnom Penh Studio

I've been mentally taking notes for a Peter Klashorst profile for years. I haven't had writer's block so much as a dam of ideas broken open to a whole torrent of thoughts, making it hard to decide which stream of consciousness to follow. Klashorst as artistic genius is the easy choice. There are many others from which to choose. For those unfamiliar with the Dutch painter who in the 1980s became one of the leading personalities of a European art movement named "The New Wild Ones" I hope to introduce a small part of him to you. For those of you who know Peter better than I, my goal is to weave a partial portrayal of him that will be worth reading. I'm not adverse to seeking advice when I find myself in deep water so I asked a writer-friend how he would describe Peter. "That's like asking a blind man to describe an elephant", he replied. That pretty much describes the task at hand for me. I asked another man of accomplishment to describe Peter in three words. My assumption was I'd get back three adjectives. There are thousands applicable to Peter. Instead he returned, "A train wreck." That response caught me by surprise yet I understood how the phrase applied instantly. Peter Klashorst would be a difficult person to come across without taking a longer look. He's a physically small man with a big heart and a steam engine of a libido, when he's healthy, along with carloads of impressive art to his name.

My personal struggle with his profile always came down to a simple question. How do I separate the artist from the art? That seems to be the popular course in the #metoo times of Bill Cosby, Harvey Weinstein, and Woody Allen. Then I read a line on British author John Burdett's Facebook page that got me on the right track. John wrote about a lifetime observation of his that "…great talent and conventional morality rarely inhabit the same body." That made me think. A lot. For one, what is "conventional morality"? I'm not sure. But I am reasonably sure that Peter Klashorst's morality is unconventional. He is also, unequivocally, a great talent. I'm sticking with artistic genius. Let's define it:

Genius: Very great and rare natural ability or skill, especially in a particular area such as science or art. – Cambridge English Dictionary

How many artistic geniuses with unconventional moralities have you met in your lifetime? I've met damn few that I know of. And I think I know why. I'm not always eager to meet them. That was the case for me with Peter. Four friends were heading over on a Sunday evening to meet-up with the painter and I was invited along. I gave it a pass. Pablo Picasso may not have been called an asshole, but I figured Peter likely was one. Anybody that talented must be. So why meet him? Life is short.

A photograph of Peter Klashorst by Robert Mapplethorpe
(Image may be subject to copyright)

However, Peter's art continued to intrigue me. So I decided to buy a Klashorst original. If you are going to be a consumer, as we are taught to be in the USA, you might as well be a creative one. And besides, the price was right.

Peter was once photographed by the famous photographer Robert Mapplethorpe when he was a younger and already a highly established artist well known in the New York City art scene and the larger art world. Peter won the Buning Brongers Award, a biennial Dutch art prize for young artists, which is the biggest private art prize of the Netherlands. In 1983 he received a prestigious Dutch Royal Award from Queen Beatrix. If that doesn't impress you I heard from a credible source that he was the first choice to do an artistic re-branding of Heineken beer bottles and beer cans until that unconventional morality got involved. None of this information was known to me at the time I met Peter in

December of 2015 at Hemingway's Bangkok to conclude my purchase. I just knew he was good at what he did. You don't need to be an art expert to figure that out.

Peter arrived wearing flip flops, jeans rolled up with self made three inch cuffs, a denim collared shirt untucked, no jewelry or watch, and a pale white chrome dome. His body was smaller than I had visualized but nothing else about him or his personality was diminutive. References provided upon request.

We sat down and ordered reasonably good food – oysters and sushi. It was the afternoon, so Peter drank water as we ate and talked. The alcohol comes later, at night, he told me. Peter is immediately likable. That caught me off guard. I'm convinced that had art not been his calling he would have made a fine Bentley car salesman on Wilshire Blvd in Los Angeles. First Round draft choices of the Lakers or Clippers and the rich and famous would all find Peter's charm and selling ability genuine. Like his art it wouldn't be a question of whether you are going to buy from Peter but which one? Peter would hate that job, of course, as he would any conventional job. To my knowledge, artist is the only occupation he's ever known. Lucky guy. There is no pretense with Klashorst. What you see is what you get and truth is what you will hear. Unfiltered truth. He's a rare bird in that he doesn't come across like he's all that but he is all that. Peter took ample interest in me too (no hash tag). Bonus points.

With Peter was the painting he had completed from a smaller study he had posted online. It was a painting of his home and studio on Street 130 in Phnom Penh, Cambodia. The work was inspired by a painting completed in 1888 by another Dutch painter, Vincent Van Gogh. Titled "The Street" by Vincent but better known to art lovers as "The Yellow House." Both paintings depict the artists immediate surroundings and the place where much of their art was/is produced. I liked the painting straight away from the study, but what Peter brought was considerably more detailed. It was much better than I had hoped for. I was as happy as any material item can make a person happy. I would later learn that in October of 2014 Peter had an exhibition of his art shown at his home depicted in the painting, named appropriately, Lust for Life.

It is Peter's lust for life that makes me now realize you cannot and should not separate the artist from the art. It is a continuum. Peter is the art and the art is Peter. You can't have one without the other and the world is a more interesting place because of each. A more recent exhibition of Peter's art was held in Bangkok called Cunt and Cock Show held at Rebel Art Space. It featured, well, must I paint you a picture? Peter painted plenty. Themes found in Klashorst paintings range from the erotic, irony, death, power, absurdity, humor, politics, Disney characters, Super Heroes, paradox, junk food, society – high and low – or any combination of these.

Painting is a very personal experience. As Peter commented in an interview with the Phnom Penh Post a few years ago, "It's like showing yourself totally naked and it's terrible. You cannot run away." It's often said that art speaks to us. Peter's art has a large vocabulary – some of it obscenity laced. What you hear and see will depend on your own eyes, ears, and mind. My mind tells me that Peter is a brilliant portrait artist. In reality he's brilliant at whatever art he attempts, I just prefer some brilliance over others. So, too, does Facebook. Peter has been banned multiple times, not long ago for depicting Mickey Mouse in a sexually explicit pose with a grown woman. Facebook, in its infinite wisdom, deemed that Mickey was a child and thus Peter had depicted child pornography as art. Peter countered with an offensive that he had a copy of Mickey's Identification proving the mouse was a man. Considering that Mickey was conceived in a garage by Walt Disney in 1927 I liked Peter's chances in a court of law. But Facebook dispenses with those formalities – they are the new sheriff in town and Peter is Otis on the old Andy of Mayberry Show, the likeable imbiber always doing short-time.

There are legitimate reasons for people to want to discuss the unconventional morality of Klashorst in more detail. His trials and tribulations with HIV and the health complications that followed due to his voluntary decision to stop taking health-benefiting medications for periods of time are well documented. Read his Wikipedia page for starters. Decisions have consequences as a Yale Law School lawyer once told me. I have gone from not liking Peter Klashorst before I ever met him, to liking him a great deal, to questioning his judgment, to hoping he likes me. And none of that matters. Yes, decisions do have consequences and Peter Klashorst makes those decisions every single day. He decides to paint and engage his talent on his own terms as an act of free will. He decides to live. He will die another day. Those decisions are far reaching and long lasting. He is the embodiment of what it means to be an artist in this century or any century past. He's not the last of the Mohicans, he's still a new wild one.

Christopher G. Moore with Peter Klashorst
(Photograph by Alasdair McLeod)

After my initial two hour meeting with Peter at Hemingway's I was impressed with his demeanor and stories, so I told him, "Someone should write a biography about you." Peter replied, matter-of-factly, "Oh, they have."

Of course they have, I remember thinking. Of course they have.

CHAPTER 15

British Author John Burdett Discusses Brexit the day before the Election

Interview with John Burdett

Popular crime novelist John Burdett holds strong opinions on Brexit, and with good reason. Born in England, the creator of the best-selling detective Sonchai Jitpleecheep series divides his time between his homes in the south of France and Thailand.

A strong advocate of the UK staying in the European Union, Burdett, who worked as a lawyer in Hong Kong for 12 years, offers candid opinions on the divisive topic.

John Burdett at his home in France – a rare selfie
(Photograph by John Burdett)

KC: The Brexit Referendum, promised by UK Prime Minister David Cameron, will be held on June 23rd, 2016. It's raised global interest, and sparked the passions of British citizens around the world, as well as those living in the UK and Europe. Soon British voters will cast their votes on whether they want to stay as a member of the European Union or leave. It's a subject that interests you. What camp are you in and why?

JB: I am firmly in the remain camp, but not because I have any illusions about the European Union. I have owned a house in France for twenty years, so I know very well how rule-bound and sclerotic the system is. Everything its critics say is probably true: non-democratic, control obsessed, inefficient, run by PhD's incapable of breaking out of the world of convenient abstractions in which they reside. What the Brexiters do not acknowledge is that the UK is really not much different, but I promise that everyone brought up in the UK understands the subtext of their passion: they ferociously oppose immigration into the UK. As the former Conservative foreign secretary William Hague said in the Telegraph today (June 7, 2016), the policy of the Brexit campaign, when faced with an intelligent discussion of the economic consequences of Brexit, is to "talk about immigration quickly." However the Brexit Ego may posture, the Id is all about xenophobia. This has enabled its campaigners to attract the likes of Nigel Farage and his coven of irrational loathing.

That a bunch of old Etonians have succumbed to an atavistic mythology which puts England (read them) in an heroic light, evoking deeds of derring do in far-off and hyper-challenging lands, should not surprise us. The reality is that the only time the UK has been truly wealthy was during the period of slavery and opium trading.

Our colonial forefathers were simply world-class gangsters who thought in a similar way to the king pins of the Medaillin cartel. There is no possibility at all that the world will allow us to behave like that ever again. The last break-out from this bunch (one thinks particularly of Tiny Rowland and Jimmy Goldsmith) destroyed the British manufacturing base and brought on the hell of corporate raiding, which spread to the US and has led directly to the economic chaos of the present time. I am in the Remain camp because I am a European and it is important for the world that Europe remains intact. The Brits have forced some very useful reforms on the EU They need us, we need them.

KC: You mentioned what the Brexiters do not acknowledge – what biases might they have?

JB: While I grew up the UK turned into "the sick man of Europe." We had very little money, most people were poor compared to today. When (Harold) Wilson (UK PM 1974-76) tried to fix the inequality, he forced the country into bankruptcy and had to borrow from the IMF. It is largely thanks to Europe (which accounts for 60% of UK trade) that the country has prospered recently. It is no accident that the Leave campaign is struggling precisely because the middle-aged, middle-class vote, which would like to be in favour of leaving, has been alienated from the Leave campaign because no Brexiter has been able to come up with a coherent plan as to how the UK might continue to prosper after the exit. As I implied in my first answer, the Leave leaders are selling a highly romanticised and atavistic view of the UK, entirely for their own benefit. They want to be lords again, in the old style.

KC: President Barack Obama went to England to make his pitch as to why leaving the EU would be a bad idea. This seemed to upset a lot of people. Did it bother you?

JB: If people were upset, it's because they have trouble looking at the full picture. Many Brits suffer under the delusion that there is a special relationship with the US, which will always save us. Obama and probably the whole of the American political class want the UK to stay in Europe, because we provide a convenient commercial and political base from which America can influence Europe. Common language and customs make this a good, easy fit for both parties.

However, if the UK loses influence in Europe big time, as will certainly be the case if Brexit happens, then America will have to court another, better-placed country, which will inevitably be Germany. The switch will not cause too much disruption to the US: plenty of leading Germans are fluent in English and we can expect cadres in the State Department to learn German and/or French to fluency level if their careers depend on it.

KC: I tend to believe the bookies more than the pundits when it comes to politics. The bookies are staying at very short odds. A $3 bet will return $4.00. Have they got it right; do you feel confident there will be no Brexit?

JB: No, I do not feel confident there will be no Brexit. If I were not culturally and economically involved, I would look on the situation as a fascinating battle between Humans and Neanderthals. The mythology of the UK is its major weakness. People still think in terms of 'splendid isolation' even if the phrase is too embarrassing to confess to out loud.

As I explained above, we never grew prosperous from isolation, our greatness and fortune were based on gangster tactics overseas (emulated in their entirety by the other European empires). In reality we never were isolated. We have been part of Europe since Roman times and now the only friends we have left are in Europe. But try explaining that to an old Etonian whose fundamental conviction is that he does not want to see his village green and cricket pitch taken over by a tent city of immigrants. I am not making this up. A large proportion of the arguments in favor of Brexit make sly reference to the village green (read: the threat of immigration). This illustrates the problem of national attention deficit. The vast majority of native Brits do not have and never have had a village or a green or even a cricket pitch to live next to. We are in the same position as the immigrants. But that's not something you learn on the playing fields of Eton.

A BOOK REVIEW OF THE BANGKOK ASSET
BY JOHN BURDETT

"Concentrate on the most unpleasant death you can think of, then how it will be at the end, when you realize there never was a heaven or a morality and every single little thing you did to make your life and the world better was a total waste of time."

"Why are you so hung up on desolation?"

"It's where the treasure is hidden."

The above passage is near the end of Chapter 4 of John Burdett's 38 Chapters and latest Sonchai Jitpleecheep novel, *The Bangkok Asset* – the sixth in the best-selling series and in my opinion his best. It's taken over 10 years but i now have a new favorite, eclipsing the inaugural novel, *Bangkok 8.*

There is a lot to be enjoyed for the reader or R of this novel as Sonchai has made a subtle but important change in how he converses with readers whom he previously addressed as, DFR or Dear Farang Reader in novels past.

Technology has changed a great deal since Burdett penned *Bangkok 8* in the early years of the 21st century. The times are changing and so is the genre Burdett chooses. Or has it changed as some have claimed? To steal three words from *The Bangkok Asset,* used more than once, "I'm not sure."

Certainly the recently launched novel is Burdett's most geopolitical and "sci-fi" oriented to date but Bangkok continues to be a vital character. Fans of the series will recognize Soi Cowboy and the bar owned by Sonchai's mother, the Old Man's Club. Burdett also does a masterful job of peeling back the layers of Klong Toey Slums, or KTC (Klong Toey City) in the local vernacular. The relationship between Sonchai and his wife, Chanya continues to be a favorite for me, as Burdett balances the characters' boredom of a long marriage with friendly dick jiggles, while getting in messages of husbands being tamed and freedoms lost, often with his trademark Buddhist slant. New character, Inspector Krom, a techie expert assigned to the case, provides some tense moments, sexual and otherwise. As the well-dressed lesbian with Butch tendencies – she has more than a passing interest for Chanya.

The plot unfolds quickly with a neatly decapitated school-girl found murdered only blocks from Sonchai's District 8 police headquarters, along with a revealing but unclear blood-written message directed at my favorite Buddhist cop: "Detective Sonchai Jitpleecheep, I know who [smudge] father is." Sonchai is a luek krung or half caste as he refers to himself. His mother is Thai and his father is American. We learn more about both in this futuristic mystery

Advanced technology and learning take center stage in this novel when Sonchai, soon after, witnesses a double-murder on a boat in the Chao Phraya River during a raging storm. My attention now three times grabbed. Smart writing, dark humor, morality plays, and psychological insights are what readers of the Sonchai series have come to expect, and Burdett delivers big time, ambiguously and unambiguously, as we are introduced to the future, Burdett's future. It never stops being entertaining no matter how bleak the outlook, and the future is bleak, according to Burdett – we will not be wearing shades. This R still found plenty to enjoy during the read – those LOL moments when the accuracy of the writing makes me laugh at the grim present and darker future which awaits. The cross as the pinnacle symbol of corporate identity and "media rats" being two examples. Burdett writes brilliant and believable scenes with plenty of dialogue. He can work in a conversation about social identities and asparagus crepes and make both interesting. Be prepared for religion as mythology along with healthy doses of skepticism or more likely, outright disbelief.

The middle portion of the book takes place in a Cambodian jungle where old ex-military and a psychiatrist by the name of Christmas Bride live and re-live the ghosts and experiments of Christmas' past. Dr Bride is one of many Christ references to be found in *The Bangkok Asset* along with the devil himself. If I have a complaint with the book (I'm not sure.) it's that Burdett is a Brit and a lot smarter than me. This made me run to the dictionary at times, and even Wikipedia, to keep up with the words and historical characters, although I was pleased to recognize one Italian painter. Smart Brits can be eccentric, I have read, and Burdett fits that mold. Understanding the eccentricities is enjoyable but attention is required. On the plus side, Burdett provides interesting characters, even the short-lived ones, and their numbers are never overwhelming or burdensome for this reader.

There is much hidden treasure to be found in *The Bangkok Asset* by John Burdett, and plenty of booty in plain sight too.

CHAPTER 16

An Interview with Colin Cotterill

NOT THE USUAL ANSWERS

Colin Cotterill is the author of twelve books in the critically acclaimed Dr. Siri Paiboun series, which is set in Laos in the late 1970s after the Communist takeover, and which feature a septuagenarian coroner-detective, Dr. Siri and an offbeat entourage of misfit associates who help him solve crimes. His fiction has won a Dilys Award and a CWA Dagger in the Library. He is also the author of the Jimm Juree Series set in Thailand. In addition, Colin is a professional cartoonist and has been involved in several non-profit and humanitarian organizations in Australia and Southeast Asia.

Colin lives at an undisclosed location in the south of Thailand with his wife and six, er, make that seven well-groomed dogs. He doesn't do Facebook but his email is not hard to find if you want to reach him.

KC: Let's say you are God for a week, or alternatively, a writer of fiction. Some say it's close to being the same thing. How would you change the world?

cc: Last month I stood up to my knees in the surf and threw a bottle into the Gulf of Siam. It wasn't revenge for all the trash that's tossed up on our beach every monsoon season. It was a message. Yes, a message in a bottle. How romantic, you say. A German newspaper had asked arty people like myself to write a message for world peace and harmony, seal it in a bottle and dispatch it from the nearest body of water. When washed up and opened – hopefully two continents away rather than at the other end of our beach – the finder would contact the newspaper and the world would be united in love. Right, I didn't expect that to work either. But it did give me a chance to spread Dr. Siri's philosophy. Here's his message. Do with it as you wish.

The world is vast and I am microscopic.

I despair because micro-me cannot rid the world of all its shit.

But I have a postage stamp of land and a shovel.

So, hear my mini-battle cry.

FORGET THE PLANET

SAVE THE GARDEN

Author Colin Cotterill in the south of Thailand with a few of his dogs.

KC: Tell me about your Mom, or if you prefer, your Mum. Just enough

to make you uncomfortable. What did she teach you to do well? What did she teach you not to do?

cc: A few months after my thirteenth birthday I said 'fuck'. It wasn't the first time I'd said 'fuck' but on this occasion it was ill-timed and traumatic because I said it in front of my mother. I'd learned the word from our neighbour, Hilda who had an absentee husband, three kids and hygiene issues. Our block of terraced council houses did not lend itself to privacy and there was a lot that went on at Hilda's that my mum would have preferred I didn't pick up. The word 'fuck' was one such nasty and mum's disappointment burned into me like a brand. In the sixty-two years that my mum and I were sharing a planet I never heard her swear. Even if 'dash' crept from her cake-not-rising lips, she would look around, blush and say 'sorry'… even when she was alone. I'm not saying my mother succeeded in cleaning up my mouth. I played rugby and 'gosh' just didn't cut it when you were forearmed by a gorilla. But she did teach me restraint. She also taught me to be nice to people I didn't like (Bear this in mind, K). She was friendly to all our neighbours in our slummy little street, even Hilda. "A smile doesn't cost anything", she'd say. And when I'm riding my bicycle around the village I can always muster a free Ethel Cotterill smile. It works.

KC: You are involved in an anthology of short stories: *The Usual Santas: A Collection of Soho Crime Christmas Capers.* **What's it all about? It's November after all.**

cc: Actually, I haven't read it. I can only tell you about my role in it. A couple of years ago, Soho got in touch and suggested the project. I was busy but I immediately agreed and, at the time, I didn't know why. When I first wrote for Soho in 2004 it was really a little Mom and Pop publishing house in a crumbly old building in Chelsea. they had a full time staff of four.

Kyoko and I stopped by earlier this year on our way through New York. they'd moved, not far but certainly up. My first impression was how young the dozen or so full-timers were, how enthusiastic, how knowledgeable. I was really out of my depth. These days, I have trouble making complete sentences. I couldn't even keep up with them drinking, and that's my best card. The word they used a lot was 'family' and I guess they saw me as great-uncle Col. (all right. perhaps not great.) and they were right. they're still a family business, and I think that's why none of the writers they contacted for *The Usual Santas* refused them. Authors sign up for smaller houses like Soho because they don't want to be a line in a barcode.

KC: In 1959 Ernest Hemingway wrote a preface for a collection of his writings titled: *The Art of the Short Story*. In it he says many people have a compulsion to write. He didn't say writers he said, "people". He goes on to say, "The compulsory writer would be advised not to attempt the short story." Do you agree with Papa? Are you a compulsory writer? How is the art of writing a short story different from crafting a novel?

cc: Ernest (he prefers 'ernie' or 'ern') and I have had our differences over the years not least when discussing our personal philosophies of short story writing. He doesn't answer my emails so much since he died, but I take that to mean I win. My theory is that everyone needs to write as therapy to combat life. Not everyone can write a full length novel. It's a commitment. It's hard work. It's annoying. However, everyone has it in themselves to turn out short stories. Whether they're good or not is a moot point. It's getting that baby out of you before it rots and clogs you up that's important.

I'm not a compulsory writer. In fact I'm totally optional. I write to eat. Novels are hard work and they just show me how stupid I am. Would that I were good enough a writer to stop writing full length books. but, short stories, those I can handle. When Minotaur Books decided my Jimm Juree series would not be paying their executive golf fees and ceremoniously dumped her, I took it upon myself to keep her alive. Every two months I'm posting a Jimm case file on the net for almost no cost at all. I like her and think that profitability should not be the end all of successful writing. She has fans, so like this I can keep feeding their addiction. I can pop out all the plot ideas I was deprived of sharing by corporate editors. and, when the JJ case files catch on and go viral, I can sit in my Jacuzzi and sip Chivas and say, 'What do you know, Ern?'

KC: In addition to being an award winning novelist with a loyal following of fans you are also a professional cartoonist, and even do the odd book cover now and then. Is cartooning an affliction or pure joy? Which cartoonists influenced you when you were seventeen? Which ones interest you in your post mid-life crisis years?

cc: I've always seen myself as a cartoonist who writes rather than a writer who draws. I grew up with comics like Beezer and Beano, progressing through Mad magazine, which left me spoiled for life. I loved Gerald Scarfe's irreverent sketches of British idiocy and Ronald Searle's cruel caricatures. I've cartooned all my life. I've been close to making a good career out of it but no coconut. Fate was always ag'in me. A few years back I had it, the idea that would make me a household name; an editorial sports cartoon making fun of the day's top sporting event called 'New Balls Please'. I would syndicate it around the world. I put together a sample package with colourful Thai stamps and sent them to every English language newspaper in the world. (absolutely true) I sat back and waited for fame to knock on my door.

The packages would have arrived exactly on or a few days after 9/11/2001. Fate.

KC: What is the last biography or autobiography you have read?

cc: Next month is my writing month. For four weeks I'll lock myself up in a cave and produce the next book in my Dr. Siri series, and it's time to talk about the Vietnam war. I've been avoiding it for obvious reasons. There's lot of background reading. I've just finished two autobiographies of Americans involved in the conflict. one was *Sunsets, Bulldozers and Elephants* by Howard Lewin who went to Laos with IVS and USAID and *A Code to Keep* by Ernest C. Brace who spent 2,868 days as a prisoner of the North Vietnamese. (some time in the cell beside John McCain's.). I'm now thoroughly depressed. I've never spent a year in a bamboo cage. I did have quite a hard mattress at the OnOn hotel in Phuket once.

KC: Does writing a memoir interest you? If not, why not?

cc: Really, who'd want to read about me?

CHAPTER 17

An Interview with Christopher G. Moore
And a Book Review of *Jumpers*

Christopher G. Moore is a Canadian author who has lived in Bangkok, Thailand for nearly 30 years. His first novel, *His Lordship's Arsenal* was published in New York in 1985. Since then he has published 33 books, including the *Land of Smiles* trilogy, three books of essays including *Fear and Loathing in Bangkok*, and 16 novels in the Vincent Calvino Crime Series. *Asia Hand* in that series, won the Shamus Award for best original paperback in 2011. In addition he is the editor and contributor for the anthologies, *Bangkok Noir* and *Phnom Penh Noir*. His latest Calvino novel, *Jumpers* was released in November, 2016. He is married and maintains two homes in Thailand – one in the city of Bangkok and one he shares in the country with his dogs and a gaggle of ducks.

Christopher was first pointed out to me several years ago as he sat at a large horseshoe shaped bar, drinking an orange juice and staring up at the colorfully decorated ceiling. I introduced myself that evening and asked him a couple of questions. I have been asking Christopher questions at every opportunity since then and paying attention to his answers.

All good artists, whether they be a portrait artist or a novelist look where others fail to look. They see what few others see. They take the back roads and document the journey. Christopher's books over the years are now frozen portraits in time. And for me there have always been plenty of brush strokes that, while not particularly flattering, painted things as they were. About society, about Thai culture, and about us. He writes books worthy of reflection and he has done it again with his most recent entry in the Vincent Calvino crime series, *Jumpers*. The novel, Christopher readily admits, is part of a creative loop inspired by a portrait sitting he did for acclaimed new art movement painter Peter Klashorst. The sitting itself was inspired by a book Christopher read, *The Man in the Blue Scarf* by Martin Gayford.

The author Christopher G. Moore
with his portrait painted by Peter Klashorst

Interviewer: John Irving said, "Writing a novel is actually searching for victims." Do you agree with Irving? There are many kinds of victims found in fiction: murder victims, victims of power, victims of circumstance, exploited victims, and victims of society. What do you think readers search for in a novel?

Moore: I admire John Irving's novels. Though, I am not certain I'd agree that writing a novel is a search for victims. Our lives are filled with contradictions, paradoxes, and confusion. Does that make us victims? If it does, then the concept of victims needs substantial redefinition. The search in a novel is the same for everyone who seeks answers to questions: Who are we? What are we doing here? What is a satisfactory life? How to reconcile the creature-like person we are with the symbolic self that seemingly travels outside of our bodies? Seriously, no one has the answers. Never have had, and likely never will have any better answer in the future.

Rather than looking for the elusive and definitive answers, we cling to cultural illusions that appear to provide answers. In that way, maybe John Irving is right—we are victims seeking refuge in beliefs and myths because the alternatives are too terrifying. The current discontent, suggests people are waking up to the fact they've been lied to; it is becoming more difficult to set the ambushes and traps by business, politicians, government, media, and our rivals.

We look to books as we once looked to religion, for self-transcending drama, heroic models, and a worldview that creates the illusion that the human condition is loaded with purpose and meaning.

Interviewer: To live an adventurous life in Thailand often means not conforming to societal norms. Can you put your finger on any particular influences that caused you to leave the relative safety of Canada as a university law professor to go first to New York City and later to Bangkok where you now call home? Did you have mentors along the way?

Moore: There is a built-in tension inside all of us between experience and reflection. A life of exploring the back roads, and a life contemplating the meaning of back roads, and why we bother to explore them. The back roads, are the ones that lead out of town to parts unknown. It doesn't mean you must resign your job and leave your country in order to write. Those back roads loaded with new experiences are everywhere. But you have to search for them. And remember adventure is not risk free, and the more you plunge into the world the more likely you will run into some sharp edges and dangers. Experiences aren't always good. They can be fatal. Most of us are cowards who do what is expected, and narrow our lives down to a bite-sized comfort zone that is safe, predictable and seemingly stable.

Take a jump and plunge into experience and climb out of that pool and reflect on matters of fact—the nature of what has been experienced. We know the world through our experience of it. All reflection and no experience is arid, a dull and lifeless exercise in futility. All experience and no reflection, and we forgo meaning of how lives are shaped, our relationships formed, and our values tested. The most valuable life hack is to discover your own balanced combination of experience and reflection. A university tenured position grants status, access to power, money and influence. It is also a kind of luxury prison where the trustees are honored and admired. That said, I loved the academic life. It was a difficult decision, to leave. I wanted to roll the dice. It was a gamble. The odds were not something I rightfully calculated or understood at the time. I was lucky. Let me say that again, it turned out well for me. If it hadn't, you wouldn't be interviewing me. That's why interviews like this are a distortion of the odds. You're not interviewing a thousand other writers who tried something similar but it didn't work out.

My mentors came after the breakout. Most mentors look for that act of courage that risks a great deal before bothering to nurture another writer.

Barney Rosset and Stirling Silliphant filled the role but that was after I'd arrived in Thailand and had published a few novels. Barney taught me about the literary sensibilities upon which good fiction was built; Stirling taught me the Hollywood décor that the vast majority of people find holds their attention. I started out in a very different time. Those were the pre-Internet days. Mentors who worked with me for years are gone; they belong to another age. Technology has disrupted the idea of a mentor, apprenticeship, isolation, publishing, and author. Writers now turn to workshops and reading groups for support.

A case can be made, that in part, globalization and the Internet has made us more selfish, and there are fewer established writers and publishers willing to put in the long hours to mentor a writer. The world of legacy publishing is brutal: either a writer hits with a book or he or she is dropped. No mentors left in that world. And in the self-publishing world where hundreds of thousands of people are hoping for a breakthrough, who do they have as a role model? It is likely to be Sisyphus.

Interviewer: Is it possible to get bored living in Bangkok?

Moore: One lifetime isn't long enough to get bored. There is enough to experience in life for several lifetimes. Trust me, I know. Take to the road. Lose yourself to the experience of living. At the same time, re-read Darwin's *Origin of the Species* and every AI report, study and finding you can lay your hands on. What happens when you reach the end? No one knows. But I have a theory: Prepare yourself for an infinite journey of imagination to a place where you mingle with all the characters spilling out of all of the books in Borge's Library of Babel. And they know you by name and you become part of their never-ending story.

Interviewer: There are two words that often come up in your writing. They are cooperation and competition. May you talk about these two subjects? What have you learned about cooperation and competition in your lifetime?

Moore: What little I've learned about the pendulum swing between cooperation and competition is it acts as a kind of cultural yin and yang. As a species, we couldn't have scaled to the level of providing food, transport, education, medical care, and communication to billions of people without cooperation. The problem is cooperation appears to work best in small groups where everyone knows everyone else. They all have skin in the game and it is in their interest to cooperate. Over the past 20,000 years we competed not so much with each other but as individuals and groups against the forces of nature and predators.

If you look at infantry squads in the military, they are twelve men. To stay alive they bond, they cooperate, they watch each other's back. These tight fighting units, deployed by politicians, are psychologically closer to our original bands of brothers. Those who make the big decisions are in competition for votes, popularity, and status, and they have no problem putting a knife in someone else's back. We fight in pre-Dunbar numbers; we govern in a post-Dunbar number political system.

We live inside this contradiction without being fully aware of how group size has changed our relationships with one another. We are post-Dunbar number casualties. When is the last time a politician threw himself on to a grenade to save those around him? Get back to me on that one.

Our fears were, in other words, different from modern fears. We needed to balloon the population to go to the next stage. Once the group expanded and disappeared into large cities, the walls protected against the old enemies but they didn't protect us against ourselves. We saw ourselves differently. The world wasn't us against a tiger or lion; it was us against others like us but different. We came to view outsiders with different beliefs, values, ethnic and racial profiles as a threat to group identity. Once the dynamic driving fear changed, our behavior changed.

The irony of this shift is apparent when you look at the way we process climate change. We are back 20,000 years ago where the most immediate threat is from nature. That requires cooperation. So far all the evidence is that cooperation is difficult to scale at a worldwide level to meet the challenges of climate change. We are too busy competing for resources and the system is too profitable to shut down. If climate change reduces our species to pre-agricultural society numbers, it will be because we were frankly too good at arguing the virtues of competition.

We have forgotten how we began and how our original fears were triggered. Nature is giving us a lesson in humility and teaching us that cooperation is not a code word for loss of liberty and freedom.

Interviewer: In addition to be being a novelist you are an accomplished and prolific essayist. Your essays have appeared in the Evergreen Review among other places and can be found on your web site www.cgmoore.com. Your latest essay is about Artificial Intelli-

gence. May you talk about writing essays in broad terms? What do you get out of it personally and what do you hope to provide to those who read them? Which essayists do you read regularly?

Moore: Essays are my diversion from the world of fiction. Imagination shouldn't be contained to the realm of make believe. They are a way to reach out to others with descriptions, explanations, and speculations about a range of subjects that interest a writer. For me, my interests lead me to: AI, climate change, crime, culture, or science. A good essay is a conversation with a friend about a matter that opens us to a better understanding of our limits, potentials, and the dangers and obstacles to living and dying.

The term essays, like the term fiction, covers a broad area. My essays tilt toward cultural, political, and scientific inquires. They don't try to change anyone's opinion or influence larger debates. An essay might be on my experience at the Jaipur Literary Festival ("Drinking From A Silver Urn" to the "High Cost of Badly Paid Cops"). I've also written about the writing and publishing process as I thought it might be helpful for other writers to share my experience and ideas.

George Orwell's essays are an inspiration. Given his background in Burma and Spain, his combining novel writing with essay writing, Orwell showed the way a novelist can take useful detours into the realm of essay writing. On first reading (and they bear re-reading) Orwell's essays are like a sniper's bullet that goes straight through the heart. Before you feel the pain of the wound, he reloads and the next round slams into you. He brings us to appreciate we live in a world where no one is watching our back unless it is to figure out how to lift our wallet. We've become atomized. That condition in itself makes cooperation more difficult. People are basically afraid. Orwell explains the background of how these conditions emerge and will likely continue as long as we are a species.

I also like reading, and have learned from essays written by Christopher Hitchens, Geoff Dyer, Pico Iyer, Annie Dillard, Tony Judt and Michael Chabon.

An essay is a clue to a writer's interests and preoccupations, if not his obsessions. My essays are written during periods when I am writing a novel, and they arise from my research. Sometimes an essay is a good test run for ideas. Other times, the essay is a way for me to organize and structure my thinking around an idea, as I am curious as to what the final construction will look like once I step back.

One of my novels takes at least a year to write. By contemporary standards, that is a slow dance. An essay takes a few hours. If it takes much longer, it means I've not thought through the problems sufficiently. The feedback from readers (there are a handful) has been positive. A few people read them. With so much competition for awareness, the long essay, which I tend to write, is not in favor. That should never be a concern, as the flavor of the month shifts: fast dance, slow dance, no dancing allowed. You can never predict what will happen next on the dance floor. Most of the time you are dancing with yourself. So take the time to make certain that publication rewards the reader with insights worth returning to now and again.

A reality check is also in order. An essay in the tradition of Orwell will draw a fraction of the attention that goes to videos of funny animals, or photos of food, as we seek out what makes us laugh, what makes our mouth water. We'd rather watch funny animals than read *Animal House*. An essay about crime is like the last straggler in a marathon, and only his mom and best friend are there to cheer him across the finish line.

I recently posted on FB something called the "Cognitive Bias Codex," a chart of the hundreds of biases that *everyone* has and can't cure or avoid or overcome. Understanding the meaning of that chart may be the single most important thing for anyone regarding insight into their own limitations and those of others. It can change your life in all kinds of ways. Maybe nine people liked it. A group photo of me at a dinner table with three friends registered five times as many FB likes. And so it goes.

Interviewer: Your latest Vincent Calvino crime novel, *Jumpers* has recently hit the cyber-stores. What can you tell us about it?

Moore: Hardly a week goes past without a report of a farang suicide. A "jumper" is local slang for jumping off a balcony or rooftop. There is often a question as to whether the death was suicide. That small bit of doubt creates suspicion whether the police and other authorities are covering up a murder. Why does someone jump off a balcony? There is no one explanation that fits all. Death, like life, is complicated. *Jumpers* is about the leap between belief and faith, art and commerce, the chasm between what we wish to be true about life, and its ultimate meaning.

Every writer, if he or she lasts long enough, writes his version of the *Tibetan Book of the Dead*. After all, death is the ultimate mystery; it is the one act of nature that awaits us all. The fear of death is buried inside all of us. When a private investigator looks into a suicide victim's life and death, he is finding emotional layers that we don't often talk about. Once these issues are exposed, there is a new way of approaching the meaning of death.

Jumpers is number 16 in the Vincent Calvino crime novel series. A modern day Caravaggio, a young artistic genius from Quebec, is painting a sex worker in his Bangkok studio, where Calvino finds him. Raphael, the artist, begins as a missing person case. For Calvino, it would have been better if he'd not found this artist.

By opening that studio door, Calvino enters into a hidden world of payoffs and local gangsters. What's interesting is the globalization of art and art collectors. Raphael has a commission for a series of portraits. Most of the women he paints for the series end up as suicide victims.

Rituals of death, the myth of art, and the circulation through the underground rivers of drugs, sex, and guns delivers a look at the convergence of art and human sacrifice. It all starts with a brush, a set of paints, a vision, and the accidental encounters with members of the painter's childhood in Quebec commune.

The forces that shaped Raphael's life are powerful enough to draw into their orbit Calvino, Pratt, McPhail, and Ratana, who seek to reconcile with his death, his artistic vision, the underworld connections, and the parade of sex worker models.

Crackdown, the previous Calvino novel before *Jumpers*, came out eighteen months ago. For a series of crime novels, that is a long time between books. With each of the Calvino novels, I've sought to capture the zeitgeist of Thailand. I hope that *Jumpers* will take its place alongside the other books in the series as a record of human struggle, where the idea is that while the end is always known, the actual date of the end remains a mystery.

JUMPERS: A Book Review

Christopher G. Moore is a master teller of crime tales. *Jumpers* is #16 in the Calvino series, and as a long-time fan I am familiar with the cast of characters: Vincent Calvino, Bangkok P.I. and his "cover my back", retired Royal Thai Police General Pratt (not many friends have matching bullet wounds for looking after each other). There is also Ratana, his loyal

 secretary, and the cranky and pleasure-seeking pal, McPhail. The One Hand Clapping Massage Parlor also makes a cameo appearance or two.

Jumpers features the complex, questionable suicide of Raphael, a young and talented artist who likes to paint the working girls of the Bangkok night. Raphael had a voracious appetite for painting and women, with a little Muay Thai on the side. His appearances are a mixture of flashbacks and memories. I liked him better alive than dead, but as suicides go he went out in style. *Jumpers* came across to me as a straight mystery with plenty of components, including a freedom portrait art series that Calvino takes part in, painting forgeries, counterfeit money, Bitcoins, the omnipresent secret notebook that contains incriminating info, a well written Chinese heavy named Sia Lang, and a Hong Kong billionaire who could prove problematic for Calvino.

We learn that, "What an artist looks for is what other people hide." But it turns out the artist is hiding a great deal himself, not the least of which is a cool $750,000, which he has left in his will to the suicide hotline group where he used to volunteer. Calvino, of course, is the executor of the estate. Vincent is more brainy than tough guy these days, more likely to be found cleaning his gun than firing it, in junta-ruled Bangkok. Pratt, likewise, cannot be found playing the saxophone, but he gets in plenty of appropriate Shakespearian quotes, at one point musing that the Bard must have been a Thai in a former life. There is still plenty of action, as Calvino manages a good head slam for a TKO in a bar, with four sharks swimming in a tank overhead. Justice eventually gets carried out noir style, by the other bad guys, and there are plenty of them. Calvino concludes, "Dig deep enough down and you will find some good in everyone." That is certainly true of the philandering Rafael, and the many models who drop by to shed their clothes at his busy studio.

There were times when a story board would have been helpful to keep track of the characters and plot points, but the author does a good job of tying things up at the end, and we discover a recurring question for Vinny, that many an expat has asked himself: should I stay or should I go? Moore excels once again at deciphering the culture clash we call Bangkok. While the story is the best since *Missing in Rangoon,* it's all the message points that make a Moore novel worth the time for me. When Calvino goes, here, to visit a psychologist and counselor named Gavin, who runs the Bangkok Suicide Hotline, it's like a cerebral shootout at the I'm OK, You're OK corral.

I like the way Vincent thinks nowadays. Whether he has changed or I have changed I am not sure. As is written late in the book, "In the noir landscape of Bangkok, the default was tragedy; things rarely ended well." A possible exception is Charlie, a Golden Retriever featured throughout the novel. Charlie loses two owners to suicides in *Jumpers*, but I see a good future for him, and Vincent Calvino too.

Jumpers is a dense read full of great messages and those messages will be different for each reader. That is Moore's strength. *Jumpers* takes you on a personal and cultural journey. It leaves you with as many questions as answers, but that is quite alright with me. Dig deep into *Jumpers* by Christopher G. Moore and you will find plenty beside the default tragedies that find everyone, whether you live your life as a work of art or not.

CHAPTER 18

Interview with Queen Bee Owner
John Branton

Englishman John Branton, his wife Jum and his extended Thai family, run Queen Bee Tavern located on Sukhumvit Soi 26 directly across from the Hilton Double Tree Inn. He describes himself as a "stay at home dad" and if you have ever been to Queen Bee you understand. A live 7-nights-a-week music venue will test the mettle of any man. John Branton and staff get glowing reviews for going against the grain to keep live music alive in Bangkok. When John manages Queen Bee by walking around, you hear a noticeable, "clang, clang" sound. Some say it is from the steel ice cubes he uses daily in his whiskey drinks. I have another theory.

It is always a pleasure to have any kind of discourse with John, even though we are often divided (and confused) by our common language. He is a man on a mission and his mission never ends.

KC: You and your wife Jum run a neighborhood pub with quite a history, it was the old Tokyo Joe's, that plays live music 7 nights a week. That seems like a perfect backdrop for heaven and hell. Tell me about the heavenly parts? Take me on the road to perdition as well. It can't be all glamour and riches. Am I wrong?

Ted Lewand, Kevin Wood, John Branton at Queen Bee

JB: To be fair the history, even though fascinating, is all behind us now.

The use of the word run feels a little misrepresentative, maybe we walk the place. My favourite Queen Bee motto is "together we are stronger". Another, more in keeping with the "Fawlty Towers" school of commerce is "we admit our service is poor but at least it's slow".

More accurately perhaps, it was the new "Tokyo Joes" and in its new form, for a number of reasons, it flourished no more. I never knew its previous incarnation but I know it was a much loved "Blues Bar" when it was in Soi 24. Khun Jum has the strongest direct connection with the transitional period, where, as near as I can tell, the forced relocation of the bar was to place too much strain on the glue that once proved adequate. This is my take on it; the Tokyo Joe version of the bar came with great musicians, top staff and experienced management, the flip side of this was, it was in terms of cash flow, top heavy. Add to that the unavoidable extra costs of settling in to a new venue, and cracks appeared fairly quickly.

Pear-shaped it was (Yoda voice) and there were some fallings-out, the gentle echoes of which I can sometimes hear today. Good time to mention that Jum and Jim were not altogether happy at the parting of ways, some investors were badly hurt, feelings were not all friendly, but, and I bless Jim for this, the only reference I could find on the internet was Jim explaining the demise of the bar and saying that he "and Jum had the usual misunderstandings".

We were sorry when he passed and paid our respects and made our goodbyes in a Buddhist fashion.

Measure twice, cut once.

Heaven or Hell.

Selling stuff that people want is easy, the people aren't always easy but the style of the bar attracts educated, cultured, interesting customers ………… and writers.

You can come to our bar and sit in the corner and get quietly tired on your own but to be honest it's not what we are about. The ethos is more upbeat and our view is more along the lines of a neighborhood hub and melting pot. We support the arts, which has always been particularly important to me because of my background in education. It was a good run, over 40 years teaching and examining but I needed a change in the day to day routine. We achieve the occasional book signing, keep a dedicated Bangkok/Thailand authors shelf in the bookcase, art displays, special musical events and many groups have met here over the years including interpretive dancing, self defense, Thai language lessons, creative writing, free expert advice to mention just a few.

KC: Tell me about your own musical background, as a vocation and as a love.

JB: Music was around me during my early years but it didn't talk to me until I was 11. I have on a few occasions been told I am lucky to be able to play a musical instrument but I am not convinced, it is mostly the effort you put into something. My luck was that we had a piano and my parents could afford to send me for lessons. Some natural propensity or physical attribute definitely helps, I am sure it was a hard choice for you, horse racing jockey or basketball, but having made the choice you put in thousands of hours. Piano was quickly augmented by guitar, drums, recorder, saxophone, viola, cello and music theory, to name just the major interests. By 14 I was working with my piano teacher as an apprentice teacher. I worked many hours after school and at weekends, it was pretty much a full-time job.

I am an autodidact. I didn't enjoy school and looking back I think I was badly served, I left a reasonably good school that had failed to see that I was unable to learn the basics. At 11 years old (when we progress to the secondary school system in the UK) I did not know the alphabet, months of the year, telling the time, or times-tables, to mention just some of the basic skills that somehow I had hidden my ignorance of.

As a result of my unique apprenticeship I was offered a job teaching organ at a local music store. Did I mention organ before? No, I could not play the organ. For three months I went to the store and practiced for over 3 hours a day. The owner of the store auditioned me then we progressed to the interview. "John, have you got any qualifications?", "yes, I have an O level in", … "that's fine, you can start on Monday".

Found I was good at it, taught 7 days a week and quickly earned the store more than they paid me. I got an offer from another store after one year (still only 18 at this time) and became self-employed. I worked for the next 20 years 60 contact hours a week, studied at college and gained many teaching diplomas, marrying, having kids and a divorce.

KC What influences, good or bad, did your parents have on you becoming a musician.

JB: My father got some advice and tried out some Grieg and Khachaturian on me, it was interesting but it was the popular music of the sixties and seventies that drove me on. His family played musical instruments which was not unusual in that period, but he lost them to a flying bomb in WW2 so I never met them. My mother encouraged me a lot and she could play a little piano which she showed me right at the beginning so I must credit her as being my first teacher. She saw the effort I put into music but my father was more focused on looking for my shortcomings. It may be I satisfied them both.

KC: What brought you to Thailand initially? Why did you stay?

JB: I was working for the University of West London as an external examiner. We would travel to odd places and meet strange people who would play inexplicable versions of musical masterpieces which we then reviewed with positivity. A good job, did it for a long time. I got the phone call "John, 3 tours on offer, Malaysia, Indonesia or Thailand" my response "can I have whichever is the shorter one please?" Thailand by a day, the rest is history.

Was in Thailand for a week down South, then up to Bangkok. Walked into a bar on day one, liked it, walked into a woman day two, liked her a lot. There are many factors but the most important ones were that my little boys, who had lived with me for the past 4 years were little no more and I was starting to like doing their washing, ironing, cooking etc. When I expressed to them that I might travel a lot more, they taught me the meaning of YOLO, you only live once. My boys set me free and I found an entirely unexpected and unlooked for life right here.

KC: What's important to you in life – what have you learned? What's unimportant?

JB: Getting this transcript to you before July 1st is the most important thing in my life right now.

Using every minute I have doing things I want to and being the best person I can be, clearly room for some conflicts of interest there but that's my job.

I try not to consider what is not important, there is a clue in its designation I believe.

KC: When was the last time you took the stairs two at a time. Anything special happen that day or just business as usual.

JB: Every time you mention taking the stairs two at a time I do it just to see if I can, I can. I walk faster than most people, always walk on escalators, try not to waste any time but taking the stairs two at a time is not really my style. I suspect I can climb 100 steps without too much trouble if tackled one at a time, most likely two at a time would be too much (over 70 steps in the QB so I get enough practice).

KC: You seem like a lifelong learner to me. What are you currently learning that you'd like to talk about?

JB: Really enjoying learning Thai, I could say learning the Thai language but I do mean learning Thainess. I love the shapes of the text and the odd variations and unexpected similarities that the Thai Proverbs reveal. I am also learning about bee keeping, cashew nut trees and woodwork techniques this week. It could be a very long list, I learn many things a day but enjoy the old wise man grounding the journeyman with "I've probably forgotten more things than you will ever learn". That's about where I am, if I was a mine of information it's all been shipped out now.

KC:. How long will you do what you're doing?

JB: Answering your questions seems interminable but I should be finished before the England V Tunisia match tonight.
Or
Who told you what I am doing and who else knows?
Or
Until it gets too easy and we actually make a profit, see, I'm funny.
Or
Mostly I find that events will change in an unexpected way it will have nothing to do with what we whimsically call "choice".

"Long live Queen Bee."

CHAPTER 19

Joe Cool – A Profile of Bangkok Writer Joe Cummings

J oe Cummings is cool. Anyone who doesn't wear a red MAGA cap can figure that out. Of course, that brings out the haters as well as the appreciators. We live in a binary, polarized world much of the time. I was in the Joe C hater camp, once. I had read that the Louisiana born and Army brat Cummings, best known for his pioneer days writing at Lonely Planet and Ronnie Wood lifestyle, didn't like many things about Americans or maybe it was America? Well, fuck him, right? I am an American. So let me not like Joe, first, even if I had never met the guy at the time.

I've changed camps, now, with the help of a quote from Voltaire:

"Appreciation is a wonderful thing. It makes what is excellent in others belong to us as well."

Let's face it, grudgingly if it makes you feel better, Joe Cummings does a lot of things well and worse yet he's made a good living and a good life for himself during his lengthy one-man show. Who does he think he is, making money from writing? No one does that anymore or so it seems. Joe's a self-admitted 1%er when it comes to writing – I'm less sure about his portfolio. On top of that the guy wanders all over the planet he helped emancipate and never gets lost. There was a time when I used to think that, with a break here or a chance meeting there, Joe Cummings could have been Anthony Bourdain – all whiskey wishes and raw ant-egg salad dreams. Like so many times in my life I got it ass-backwards. With a few different decisions made, perhaps Tony could have traveled a more content and longer path? We'll never know. Game Over for Bourdain. Joe's and Keith Richards' lives keep streaming on, with a few tolerable demons along for the ride.

I've read a fair amount of Joe Cummings' work. Who hasn't picked up one of his many over-priced coffee table books in a bookstore and perused it for a good-long while before setting it back down and then moving on? My favorite is, *Sacred Tattoos of Thailand – Exploring the Magic, Masters* and *Mystery of Sak Yant*. Joe did the writing and Dan White, who died too soon in 2012, created the photographs. I was too cheap to buy the book but it gave me a lot of pleasure. Mainly because it was so superior to the competition out there. You can also watch Joe do a TedX talk, filmed in Chiang Mai titled "Spells & Sigils: The Magic & Mastery of Thai Sacred Tattoos." Joe explains that tattoos, once the domain of sailors, circus performers, and gangsters, have a very spiritual, protective nature in Thailand. They've also moved upstream into HiSo/Celebrity territory.

My regular reading of Joe Cummings includes his monthly column in Bangkok 101 Magazine, appropriately titled "Joe's Bangkok." Joe's writing often times reminds me of a professional baseball umpire calling a perfect game. Joe's great at what he does. He calls the balls and strikes of any story flawlessly, and as he sees them, yet at the end of the game or in his case the article or book, you haven't noticed that he was there. He rarely becomes an integral part of the story. The reason you don't notice him is because he never makes a mistake. It is what I think makes him that rarest of things in the scribe world – an in demand writer. His latest book, which I have not read is, "The Hunt Bangkok." It's a book that helps you experience the sprawling metropolis of Bangkok the way the locals do.

I've come to believe that while Joe C is no regular Joe his spirit and mine have a lot in common besides our surname. In fact it's eerie, the amount of commonalities we share. Almost in a Lincoln/Kennedy kind of way. Here are just a few:

Joe Cummings receiving a protective tattoo in the same placement he later recommended to Anthony Bourdain

Joe Cummings holds a Master's degree from Cal Berkeley.

I was born in Berkeley, California.

Joe Cummings speaks and reads Thai language fluently.

My wife speaks and reads Thai fluently.

Joe Cummings is beanpole thin.

I used to be beanpole thin.

Joe's dad was a Golden Gloves boxer with an undefeated record.

My dad took me to a Golden Gloves boxing match once.

Joe Cummings plays regularly in a band at live music venues.

I listen to bands regularly at live music venues.

I could go on but you get the idea. Like most people we are more alike than we are different.

I did finally meet Joe long after becoming Facebook friends, at a live music pub run by an amiable Brit. Prior to that chance meeting our chats were always cordial and Joe was always helpful when I needed help. I respect our similarities and our differences. Our musical tastes don't always align but even here Joe comes across accommodating enough. On the subject of music he wrote recently, "Critics be damned. You like what you like. " It's a good attitude and I suspect it applies to Joe for critics of all kinds.

One of the subjects I chatted with Joe about was interviews. He's on record as stating that he doesn't do many. And that seems to be the case. For a guy who has shown the Bangkok ropes to the likes of Mick Jagger and Steven Tyler and tailored those threads accordingly, Joe would make anybody's interview A list in Southeast Asia. I thought of asking Joe for an interview but concluded that that would put him in a position of having to say, yes or no. And thoughtful guy that I am, I decided to spare him that choice.

It hasn't kept me from coming up with some questions I would like to ask Joe, however, so here goes. My phantom interview with Joe C.:

KC: Your father was Colonel Cummings in the Army. You were a free spirit during the Vietnam War. How were you similar to your dad and how were you different? Tell me a poignant father/son story about conflict. Tell another father/son story about bonding, please.

JC:

KC: When you graduated from Berkeley you were said to have had at least two job offers: one from the CIA and one from Lonely Planet. Tell us why we shouldn't believe that you accepted both simultaneously? It worked for the Paris Review after all.

JC:

KC: Name your three favorite guitar players whom are living and your three favorite that have died and what you like, specifically, about each, musically or personality wise.

JC:

KC: Who is your tailor in Bangkok and where do buy your shoes? What was the occasion for your last tailored suit?

JC:

KC: Where, if anywhere, did Anthony Bourdain go wrong? What were your thoughts and feelings when you heard the news?

JC:

KC: What exercise do you do besides walking? Alone, I mean. What's your best tip on how to drink alcohol and remain thin?

JC:

KC: Do you ever regret picking up the cigarette/whisky combo habit or do you wax philosophical like Christopher Hitchens used to?

JC:

KC: What were your last meals under $3.00 and over $100.00 and where were you?

JC:

KC: Do you prefer asking questions or answering questions? Why?

JC:

KC: Musicians or chefs in Bangkok. Who are the bigger rock stars? Name a maestro or two.

JC:

KC: What music streaming service do you use and recommend?

JC:

KC: What's your favorite live music venue in Bangkok, Chiang Mai, Hanoi, Jakarta, Rangoon, and Bali?

JC:

KC: What's the dumbest question you've ever been asked in an interview, this question and this interview excluded.

JC:

KC: Heaven, reincarnation, or, this is it? Choose one and tell me why it's preferable to the others.

JC:

Thanks, Joe. Lets do this again sometime. I'd ask you a question about why you don't like America, but your answer would make too much sense.

This, of course, is not the greatest Joe C interview ever. That was to get the attention of your eyeballs. That interview was done by Joe's longtime friend and fellow All-Star musician, Keith Nolan in 2016, It's part of Keith's "Beyond the Lines" series found on YouTube and aired in the past on cable television in Bangkok. Truth be told, I like to interview authors but I don't always enjoy or even watch the "Beyond the Lines" interviews. Listening to authors talk about their books can be a drag. I prefer their written words. However, this is my favorite interview in the series. It comes across as two friends, musicians, and adventurers having a good time.

Dizzy Dean is credited with saying, "It ain't braggin' if it's the truth." Satchel Paige, another baseball player, famously said, "Don't look back. Something might be gaining on you". I like Joe Cummings for a lot of reasons. Mostly because he tells the truth and doesn't look back. They are good rules for living. While others, including me, are arguing the merits or demerits of an inconsequential person or moment, Joe is just as likely to be flying into a Chiang Rai airport in a 12-seater prop plane in order to visit a biker-buddy at his bar. Joe knows. He knows what's important and what's not important. To him. And I think that is way cool.

CHAPTER 20

An Interview with Journo Pro and Maeping Mango Resort Owner David Armstrong

Career journalist David Armstrong has led and is still leading an interesting life. He is currently living in Kamphaeng Phet, Thailand. At my request, he agreed to reflect and comment on his experiences, the good luck and bad, spanning nearly fifty years. It is no small task, and I thank him for the opportunity.

KC: When I was a boy I was a regular viewer of the television series, Superman – starring George Reeves. I never wanted to be Superman; I wanted to be like Perry White. You have actually lived my dream. Can you talk about the highlights of your career in the newspaper business, beginning with your Jimmy Olson days, including the different Metropolis cities you worked in?

DA: I was keen on the old Superman series, too, but I liked the Clark Kent role: no matter what he did as Superman, he still had to rush back to the office, hit the typewriter and file a story. But I didn't aspire to be either Perry White or Clark Kent. I went to university to study medicine. The examiners, however, thought I would be better off if I studied something else. So I started on a liberal arts degree, majoring in history.

I think two key factors in my career were luck and persistence. You need more than whatever talent God gave you. My first piece of luck came in 1969, when I was appointed editor of the university newspaper (called *Tharunka*, which is an Australian Aboriginal word meaning message stick). The really lucky part involved a newspaper, called *The Australian,* which Rupert Murdoch had set up in 1964. The paper was trying to develop readership among academics and students, and a small part of their strategy was to offer a modest scholarship to the editor of *Tharunka.* And that led to a job as a junior reporter on *The Australian.* I had wanted to work on *The Australian,* as it was a national paper, dealing with big issues – not parish-pump stories like the city papers. I spent the next 15 years reporting and editing with *The Australian* and a news-magazine called *The Bulletin,* that was an Australian equivalent of *Time* or *Newsweek.* Like *The Australian,* it dealt with national politics, the economy, the arts, international news and business.

In 1985, I was appointed editor of *The Bulletin,* published by the late Kerry Packer's Australian Consolidated Press. It was a great job: the magazine was more than 100 years old and had a national reputation as the publisher of great Australian authors, poets, artists and cartoonists.

But it wasn't to last. In 1986, Kerry appointed a new editor-in-chief of the company's magazines and he thought *The Bulletin* should be turned into a lifestyle magazine. In a moment of candour, I told him I disagreed and, if that was what he wanted I probably wasn't the right person for the job. He was to come to the same conclusion. I left.

That was bad luck, but I also had some good luck. While working at *The Australian* I had grown close to News Corp's Australian chief, Ken Cowley, who was Rupert's right-hand man. Developing a friendship with Ken was the biggest single piece of good luck in my career.

Through Ken I was offered a job as a political commentator in the Sydney *Daily Telegraph.* The parish-pump stories turned out to be not so boring after all, especially when I could scoop the rival *Sydney Morning Herald.*

But Ken had other plans. In 1989 he asked me to go back to *The Australian*, this time as deputy editor.

Towards the end of the year, Ken fell out with the editor, who was removed and re-assigned as a columnist. I was appointed editor, the first journalist to start his career at *The Australian* to move on to the top job.

At that time News Corp also owned the *South China Morning Post* in Hong Kong. Ken and Rupert decided to offer me the job there when it was next due to fall vacant. But first, there was another task.

Ken and Rupert were close to Kerry Stokes, the owner of the Seven television network. Kerry also owned the *Canberra Times* and wanted to appoint an editor from the outside, to bring in some different ideas. So I was sent on "loan" to Canberra for 12 months. I loved that job: producing a national newspaper with a small team (Canberra was not a big city), relying on their enthusiasm, skills and hard work. It was fabulous.

In 1993 I went to Hong Kong – a great adventure. *SCMP* was a paper with a strong local and international reputation, and it was a time of immense change in Hong Kong and China. I had been there six months or so when Rupert sold the paper to the Kerry Group, under Robert Kuok. Robert asked me to stay on and I did. After a while the job was upgraded to editor-in-chief of the daily and Sunday papers. But the role had a time limit on it. When I was appointed my late wife, Deb Bailey also got a big job, as managing editor of the Australian edition of *She* magazine. We decided to try to manage a long-distance marriage, visiting each other as often as possible. We did it but it was very hard. If I had known Deb was to die a few years later, at the young age of 48, I would not have gone to Hong Kong.

After three years I went back to Sydney, where Ken Cowley asked me to go back to *The Australian*, as editor-in-chief. I did the job for more than 5 years, but Deb died in 2001, and although I pushed on I didn't have the strength or the energy to continue for much longer. The next year, I stepped down.

And that, I thought, would be the end of my newspaper career. I took on a corporate role with News in Sydney but in 2003 Ean Kuok, the chairman of the SCMP Group, asked me to come back to Hong Kong, as group editor-in-chief. I thought if I worked in HK for three years or so, I could build up a decent retirement bank. At that time, SCMP was a big investor in Post Publishing in Thailand, the Bangkok Post company. Post Publishing was without a permanent managing director: one of the board members was filling in until they could find one. In 2005, a deal was done to make me effectively managing director in Bangkok, while having a role called editorial director in HK, splitting my time between the two cities. After a year or so, however, SCMP decided it wanted a full-time editor-in-chief again, while I now found I wanted to stay in Bangkok. So I parted company amicably with my friends in Hong Kong. I continued as managing director until the end of 2008. It was more or less retirement time, although I did spend two fascinating years as chairman of the Phnom Penh Post company and some time as a consultant to the Myanmar Times company.

In the meantime, I had met and later married Nichapa. And that led to a new career.

KC: Looking back at your tracks, pick one decade that you would consider the most newsworthy or news-filled one. What were the stories that stand out during that 10-year period? They can be major ones that everyone would recognize and/or an important one for you personally.

"We had a dress circle seat for a play called History".
– David Armstrong

DA: Decades don't start with years ending in "1" and finish with years ending with "0". When we think of the 60s, for instance, we think of the explosion of rock music, rock concerts, sex, dope, student protests and all-you-need-is-love. But that era didn't really get underway until about 1963, when rock and the changes it spawned pushed pop aside and got rid of a lot of the starch and stiffness of the 50s. So my best decade professionally began in 1993, when I went to Hong Kong to edit the *South China Morning Post*. There, it was not so much a matter of individual stories that stand out as two big long-running stories: the brawling between Britain and China over the return of HK to Chinese sovereignty, and the emergence of China as an economic powerhouse. We had a dress circle seat for a play called History.

One of the challenges was to work out how the newspaper could play a constructive role, for HK and for China, as the handover approached. We were told the paper was influential, that it was read by some important people in Beijing. If true, it meant *SCMP* was being read by people who would not react kindly to direct criticism. We decided we would work by explanation and persuasion, doing a lot of editorials on why HK was different and why China's approach would be unproductive or counter-productive.

One of our lines was that China should not be so belligerent and negative towards HK, that it was going to inherit a great jewel and it should be reassuring the HK people and trying to be positive about tackling some of the problems it saw. I took some satisfaction when China started to calm down as the handover drew nearer. Undoubtedly, their own common sense got them there but I like to think we may have played a small part in Beijing's deliberations.

When I went back to Australia, many of the big stories seemed to involve indigenous matters. One was a High Court judgment that junked the convenient notion that Australia before the British arrived was *terra nullius* – that no one owned the land – opening the way to more extensive Aboriginal land rights. Another big story was a report into the stolen generations, a reference to the practice, in the not-so-distant past, of removing Aboriginal children from their families. I was proud of our original reporting into problems in indigenous communities, such as domestic violence and the young lives wasted by glue or petrol-sniffing. These were no-go areas for some in the media, who saw this kind of reporting as demeaning (if not defamatory) for Aboriginal people, rather than as a necessary first step in helping to tackle the problems. We also had the first Government decision to turn back migrant/asylum seekers trying to get to Australia by boat – an issue that still inflames passions in the country.

There were, of course, some very big international stories, including the death of Princess Di, the dotcom crash, the Bali bombings, and the tragedy of 9/11 and its aftermath. And one of the most exciting stories in that time was the Sydney Summer Olympics in 2000, two weeks literally of fun and games.

One story that had immense personal meaning was printed in The Australian in 2003, closing off the decade for me. My wife Deb had died in 2001 of motor neuron disease (ALS, or Lou Gehrig's disease). I subsequently gave a talk on caring for a terminally ill loved-one. In 2003 we set up a foundation in Deb's name, and *The Australian*, under Chris Mitchell, the new editor-in-chief, ran an edited text of the talk. I got more comments on that than on any story I had written during my career.

KC: You educated me regarding headline type used in the serious newspaper industry vs tabloid journalism but I am still curious, what is the tallest headline you ever had during that 10-year period?

DA: *The Australian* and the *South China Morning Post* were both broadsheet newspapers and tended to have modest headline styles. Often the main headline was only 60-point (0.83 of an inch) although we did range up to 96-point (1.3 inches). But when Aboriginal athlete Cathy Freeman won the 400m gold at the Sydney Olympics, we gave the next day's front page a magazine treatment: a full broadsheet page with just one picture – Cathy with her medal. I suspect the heading was more than 96-point that day.

KC: Let's fast forward to present day. You've decided to build and operate a resort on the Ping River in Thailand with the able assistance of your wife, Nichapa. That must make many of your friends think you have figured out the ideal way to live the good life in Thailand. Then again, some friends might think you have gone crazy? Tell me about operating a resort in Thailand.

DA: I can see why people might have either perception, but I think I'm very lucky.

Just to correct the record: it is my brilliant wife Nichapa who has built and now runs a resort and restaurant by the Ping River in Kamphaeng Phet, a World Heritage area halfway between Bangkok and Chiang Mai.

Nichapa is a fabulous cook and she is also an accountant by training, and worked as a logistics officer for two international IT companies.

She supervised the construction and now runs the operation – the restaurant and the resort. Nichapa comes from Kamphaeng Phet and we bought the land in 2008. We started building at the end of 2013 and opened two years later.

After about a year, the owner of the construction company we were using pulled out to work on other projects. So Nichapa managed the project from then on – in detail.

Are we (or I) nuts? Nichapa is working very hard, but she has a job that uses the full range of her skills and she is doing it very well. I am the support act.

Nichapa and David on a trip to Bangkok

We have a house by a wide expanse of river, in a beautiful garden setting. I have breakfast sitting on the veranda, watching the sun rise and the river flow by. At night, I get a table in a riverside restaurant and eat some of the best food in Thailand. I spend most of my time in Kamphaeng Phet. My original plan, in 2008, was to split my time between the resort and Bangkok. Since then, I have grown eight years older and the communications have become eight years better. So I'm not isolated. I also have a few tasks, like managing social media and the website, that give me something to do, something to keep my brain ticking over, in my declining years. This is important to keep me occupied, as I can't play golf.

Aerial view of Maeping Mango Riverside Resort
shortly before the opening

One of our guests said Maeping Mango was a perfect place in which to do nothing. He meant it kindly: that the garden is peaceful, the river is calm and soothing, the air is fresh, there's no noise and the food is first class. You can decide if that's crazy.

CHAPTER 21

Interview with Lefty Award Winner Tim Hallinan and Book Review of The Hot Countries

Timothy Hallinan is the Edgar-, Shamus-, and Macavity-nominated author of sixteen widely praised books, including *The Fear Artist*, *For the Dead*, *Crashed*, *Little Elvises* and *Herbie's Game*, winner of the Lefty Award for Best Humorous Crime Novel. His seventh Bangkok thriller in the Poke Rafferty series is, *The Hot Countries*. After years of working in the television and music industries, he now writes full time. Tim divides his time between California and Thailand.

KC: Let's talk characters in the Poke Rafferty series – Poke, Rose and Miaow. Of the three Miaow is your favorite. Who is Miaow?

TH: I really see the series as having a triple protagonist: the members of a makeshift family, three people with literally nothing in common—an American travel writer, a former bar worker, and a little girl who was abandoned on the sidewalk at the age of two or three. They all understand that this often-difficult relationship may be their last chance at home and happiness. They're in it together, so to speak.

Miaow—the adopted daughter—is based on a real child I met in the early 1990s, a gum-seller in the Patpong area, who used to stare in amazement at my laptop as I wrote in a restaurant window. Eight or nine, filthy, but with a ruler-straight part in her hair because that was the one aspect of her life that she could control. Eventually, I waved her in, bought her a Coke, set up Pinball on the laptop, showed her how to work the flippers, and took a walk. When I got back, the booth was empty, there were two packs of gum stacked neatly on my plate, and the pinball score was astronomical. I saw her dozens of times after that, until she disappeared a year or so later. Her name really was Miaow, and I put her in the books hoping that it might produce a little sympathetic magic; as things worked out for the child in the books, I hoped, some of it might shade over into the real child on the street. I actually tell the story of how I met her in *The Hot Countries*, but in the book it's Poke she meets.

When you're writing adults, three or four years don't mean much, but to a child it's an eternity. Over the course of seven books, Miaow has learned to trust her adoptive parents, she's worked her ass off to get into a good school (where she hides the shame of her past on the streets), she's had her heart broken, and now, at fourteen she's decided to be, God help us, an actress. And every day she changes a little more. I never know where she'll be in the next book.

KC: You've been described as a Charles Dickens writing about modern-day Thailand, and in fact you once wrote a book about Dickens. You also weave Shakespearean references into the Poke series. Why are Dickens and William Shakespeare considered to be great writers?

TH: The Dickens comparisons come, I think, because Dickens was the great Victorian writer of children, and there are so many kids in the Rafferty series. I think children are fascinating characters because they don't get a vote. Up to a certain point, virtually everything in their lives is determined by adults. The Rafferty books are full of kids who are getting raw deals, whether they're poor or rich.

Both Dickens and Shakespeare—certainly the greatest writer ever to work in English—had the gift of being able to see things whole: not just the street corner (or the throne room) but the complex network of fears and desires that drive what happens in those places, and at the same time they could place all that within their private understanding of how this endlessly mysterious world works. And finally, they could take whatever they wrote and make it *fascinating*. I'm thrilled to be mentioned in a sentence with Dickens, but if anyone ever compared me to Shakespeare I'd say he or she was delusional. I'd say thanks, too, of course.

KC: What books would you recommend the novice begin reading with these two greats?

TH: Start Dickens with *Great Expectations*. I'd begin Shakespeare with *Macbeth* because it's a short, hair-raising, blunt force instrument with witches and ghosts in it and the most complex female villain I've ever read. The thing about Shakespeare is to read him aloud, at least part of the time.

KC: Bangkok as a setting has many kinds of street corners. It is a city with many different looks and strata. How is writing about Bangkok different than writing about the San Fernando Valley, where your Junior Bender series is set in California? Are there any similarities?

TH: Some people define setting as place, but to me, it's *place as characters experience it*. Otherwise, I think it's a postcard or one of those painted flats that were used in 19th-century theater. What that means to me is that there are several Bangkoks in the Rafferty books. Rafferty, who first experienced it as an adult from the Western world, lives in a completely different Bangkok than Rose, who ran away to it and became a bar girl, or Miaow, who was given a big lemon ball by her parents and then tied by her wrist to a bus bench and left there, and who didn't accept that they weren't coming back until the candy was finally gone. The streets, to her, are nothing like the streets her parents experience, and that lets me write Bangkok, in a sense, in several dimensions. Of course, one of the magical things about Bangkok, from a writer's perspectives, is that it has all these kinds of people in it. You can stand on any Bangkok sidewalk and see three possible novels in five minutes.

The San Fernando Valley is the least exotic setting in the world, a one-time paradise that's been downgraded to a slurb, part slum, part suburb. But Junior Bender is a *burglar*, so the books are set in a burglar's Valley. A burglar looks very differently at a street lined with expensive houses than a guy with a map to the stars' homes does. To a burglar, a *cul-de-sac*, as Los Angeles realtors call it, is just a dead end, not a desirable place to live. So in a sense the settings of all my books are actually in the minds of the characters, and we experience those places through the characters' perspectives.

And another big difference is that I love Bangkok, and I endure the Valley.

KC: The original expats who came to Thailand after the Vietnam War got older. You write about those original expats in *The Hot Countries*. What did you learn about them?

TH: When I wrote the first Rafferty book, *A Nail Through the Heart*, I came up with a little dump called the Expat Bar, loosely modeled on the old Madrid on Patpong One. The idea was that all the old Bangkok Hands gathered there and complained about the way the city had changed. They were kind of comic and sad at the same time. I used them in several books, and then about four years ago I read a line of Sappho: *He was handsome then and young, but soon gray age overcame him, the mortal husband of an immortal wife.* It was like a bolt of lightning. The guys in the bar have gotten older, but the girls in the street, their "wives" in a manner of speaking, have remained the same age. They're not the same girls, but they're the same age. And I knew there was a book there. These were strong, decisive guys, adventurers, exposed over time to a particularly cruel metric: losing their beauty and vitality among all that youth and seeing their faltering present-day selves reflected in those uninterested eyes.

But, as the villain of that book finds out, they're not to be underestimated.

KC: There's a kind of preview of part of *The Hot Countries* in the anthology, *Bangkok Noir,* first published in 2011. It's a story about Wallace. How did that come about?

TH: I was thinking about the story that would become *The Hot Countries* (in a very different form) when the inestimable Christopher G. Moore emailed me to ask if I'd like to contribute a short piece to that book. I'd only written one short story since eighth grade, and I tried to beg off, but then Wallace came to mind and I took a fragment of one way my book might conceivably have gone and wrote it as a story called "Hansum Man," unwittingly ripping off Dean Barrett. Much to my surprise, people liked it. And part of that story is in *The Hot Countries*, but framed differently and with a different ending. So having read the story doesn't let you off of reading the book.

I'd like to say one thing before I go. On the surface, Bangkok is not the city that I first saw in the 1980s, when parts of it deserved the descriptive phrase Somerset Maugham applied to Monaco, "A sunny place for shady people." Now it's a world-class city in every regard, and yet its *spirit* seems to me to be the same, a unique and almost musical mixture of the sublime and the appalling. "A man who is tired of London is tired of the world," as Dr. Johnson said, and in the 21st century, I think that's true of Bangkok. I can't imagine ever running out of things to write about it.

Count your blessings. That's my best summation of *The Hot Countries* by Timothy Hallinan. Recognize them, count them, hold onto them, and appreciate them before it's too late or worse yet, before you die.

Poke Rafferty is a tougher than usual travel writer who is also a family man capable of crying during a television commercial designed to jerk tears or when his daughter performs brilliantly in a school play production. He is part of a

diverse expat community living in Bangkok, Thailand. By choice many of his friends are aging longtime expats, holdovers from the Vietnam War era. Hallinan is a gifted writer and one of those rare authors capable of putting out two novels per year for two separate and successful series. The other being his Junior Bender series set in Southern California. Both series have drawn the attention of a number of the more prestigious book awards, as any mantel or bookshelf in his home could surely prove. There was a time when you would see A BANGKOK THRILLER stamped on this series of books but that is no longer the case. In its place you now see A POKE RAFFERTY THRILLER. That's a subtle but appropriate change.

A Hallinan novel is always character driven and *The Hot Countries* is full of characters you will recognize, and ones you will hope to avoid for a lifetime. Bangkok as a character is still there to be appreciated but she's been pushed into the wings to play a supporting role. As this novel notes, expats are drawn to the hot countries, and this expat tale could have been written successfully with any number of them serving as the backdrop because the writing and story are what hold your interest.

Some characters are too good to kill off and others are so good you need to bring them back from the dead. So it is with Treasure, a 13 year old girl psychologically damaged from the abuse of her nightmarish father, Murphy, and Wallace, an elderly and forgetful veteran, (Wallace first appeared in the short story Hansum Man found in the 2011 anthology *Bangkok Noir*). Wallace remembers a Bangkok that has long ago disappeared. He once served time in Leavenworth for desertion and now longs to recreate the memories of bar girl love which deserted him.

The meeting place for these expats is called the Expat Bar. It is at this bar that Hallinan gives us some of his best writing, which leaves the reader pondering some of life's great questions: how should someone spend a life? How much would you do for those you love? How much would you do to save the lives of people you hardly know? How bad can a bad man be? I particularly liked the description of an interrogation room with a drain meant to be noticed and the dramatic usefulness of chicken blood.

The Hot Countries is the third in an informal trilogy starting with *The Fear Artist,* where the focus is more on Poke going it alone as a fugitive with the help of his Thai Royal Police friend, Arthit, and the follow-up, *For The Dead*, which focuses more on Poke's family, wife Rose and adopted child Miaow. Mia, as she is known to her school mates, is an aspiring actress, also 13 years old, and is put center stage in more ways than one. This is a novel with more suspense and familial moments than thrills, as Poke does what he does best, protect his family (which has made him whole) from the worst men that war societies have created.

Treasure becomes a desired pawn, in a power play of greed and evil on one end, and love and generosity on the other. Miaow, being the same age as Treasure, becomes the conduit of both desires, showing her hard-earned wisdom, achieved from knowing what it is like to be abandoned and then wanted at an early age. Miaow teaches Treasure that finding people who love you is only part of the equation in life's journey, "You have to say yes. You have to let them love you." Hallinan pays homage to all the right people, places and things in *The Hot Countries,* including his fellow authors, Christopher G. Moore in Chapter 1 and Dean Barrett in the Afterword.

After seven novels in this series, Tim Hallinan still possesses that ability most coveted by published authors: he makes you want to turn the page. If you are looking for a great Bangkok Thriller then I highly recommend the fourth in the series *The Queen of Patpong.* If you want to read a very good novel that happens to have a lot of ageing expats in it, no matter what demographic category you may be in, even if you've never been to Thailand, then read *The Hot Countries,* published by SoHo Crime. Whether you are on a beach in Rio De Janeiro, or waiting for winter to end in Calgary, Canada or expecting a child in Azusa, California, *The Hot Countries* will make you think about life and what it takes to create one.

CHAPTER 22

Interview with Collin Piprell

Collin Piprell is in the business of generating alternate realities and then exploring them. He's a Canadian writer and editor based in Bangkok. He's also lived in England where he did graduate work at Oxford, and in Kuwait, where he learned to sail, water-ski, and make a credible red wine in plastic garbage bins. He's written books and articles about diving, boating, coral reef natural history and wining and dining. His novels include, *Kicking Dogs, MOM* and *Genesis 2.0.*

KC: You've seen it all and done it all. On land, sea, and air. An elephant tracker, a miner, a scuba diver, and paraglider.

CP: Although I have followed elephant tracks, I'd hesitate to call myself an elephant tracker.

KC: I'd rather hear about the dangers of being a traditionally published author in the 21st Century. You've got a new book out. Tell us about *MOM*. I hear it's now a series.

CP: *Genesis 2.0,* the second in the series is already available, and *Resurrections,* the third, is in progress. The fourth and fifth novels are notes and bits of draft plus a source of disquiet when I awake late at night to review the state of the world.

 MOM kicks off around AD 2057. Feral self-replicating nanobots have very nearly brought about the extinction of the entire biosphere, including the human race, and the last two refuges – Eastern Seaboard USA Mall and Eastern Seaboard SE Asia Mall – are under siege.

 Behind the story of how a few humans manage to survive the PlagueBot, we find another story: a war between the machine mall operations manager (MOM) and Brian Finister, the human MOM she superseded, a 113-year-old who remains invisible to her in a hideout concealed in part by selectively blinding her with bugs he left in her operating system before she came to self-consciousness. So the machine MOM covertly recruits our heroes to help her home-in on her human foe.

 And behind that thread there's yet another tale, one that unfolds more clearly in the second and third novels – i.e. the emergence of novel evolutionary developments as significant as the earlier emergences of life, perception and motility, and the subsequent rises of intelligence, language use, culture, artificial intelligence and generated realities.

 Ironically enough, the PlagueBot – the global superorganism that arose from the new grey-goo scenario – itself becomes one element of the basis for a human renaissance within a renewed, though radically different kind of biosphere.

 That may sound way too stodgy. In fact these novels present lively, even funny, reads that focus on dramatic conflicts between a motley cast of characters. *MOM,* e.g., presents a story of elaborate revenge. Here's a teaser, something from Leary, one of the characters (see below):

The Inuit, what we used to call Eskimos, they had a trick. An early kind of trojan. They'd bend a piece of sharpened whalebone over, wrap it in blubber, tie it up tight with something and freeze it. Then they'd take the string off the bait and leave this nice surprise lying around for a polar bear to find. The bear would see it, hardly believing its good luck, and wolf it right down. The blubber would thaw out way down there inside his gut and the whalebone would spring open. After a while the bear would bleed to death, or at least slow down enough the Inuit hunters could catch up and kill him some other way.

Genesis 2.0 takes up where *MOM* ends, from a new character's point of view. Before too long, we also encounter the surviving cast from *MOM*. It turns out Brian Finister is still at war with the machine MOM, but the story becomes complicated when one of MOM's ugly stepsisters, a totalitarian personality alter that gains the ascendency, establishes herself as the new villain of the piece. This entity, whom Brian has dubbed "Mildread" after one of his exes, really comes to the fore in *Resurrections.*

KC: What's the upside (if there is one) and the down side to the digital age we live in for writers in particular and the human race, such as it is?

CP: The internet and 24/7 connectivity by way of our gadgetry can give us a godlike feeling that we're parked at the hub of the universe with All That Is right there at our fingertips. If you're a working freelancer, for example, you can't understand how anyone ever got along without it.

But our machines are fast learning how to do much of what has traditionally been reserved to humans. Already there are programs that churn out routine journalistic pieces and company reports and so on, a development that can leave us wordsmiths feeling less godlike.

And there's another downside to our enthusiasm for digital gadgets and the internet. We're steadily outsourcing what we've always thought were essentially human capacities, and it's quite likely we won't recover some of them. Again, I've blogged on this issue, for example with "Outsource our minds? What a good idea!" (www.collinpiprell.com).

KC: Do you have a routine?

CP: Wish I could say I did. I believe that straight out of bed to the writing in the morning is the best way to go. For sure you should go nowhere near the internet till you've spewed some hours of words. But given my basically undisciplined nature plus too many other commitments at any given time, I write when I can. Sometimes that's straight out of bed, but not often enough.

KC: You once wrote a lot while you were at sea. Tell me about that experience. Were there distractions or was it pure bliss?

CP: I once worked some fragments up into a complete novel in draft during nine weeks on a derelict yacht between Israel and Thailand. I did this against all odds, against my own belief it wouldn't be possible.

I really enjoyed the experience, but I wouldn't describe it as bliss. I was doing odd jobs and standing watches all the while, and after a work crew in Cyprus stripped some cabins, mine for example, so they could patch a bunch of holes in the steel hull, I had nowhere to call my own to work or sleep. and, by the time we hit the Red Sea, the temperatures were ranging to around 50 degrees C and rather higher in the engine room. Nothing worked – not the air-con, not the fans, only the twin Gardner diesels, a pump or two and my laptop.

But yes, I do work well on boats.

KC: Tell us about your body of work to date.

CP: DK Books published my first book, *Bangkok Knights,* way back when I was still teaching (mostly writing) at Thammasat University. A British doctor who used to live here in Bangkok recommended the manuscript to Khun Suk, the owner of a chain of bookstores and a publishing house. Later DK also published *Kicking Dogs,* a novel. Both of those books were later picked up by bookSiam and then by Asia Books, who also encouraged me to write *Yawn: A Thriller*, which they eventually published as well.

Around the time I came up with *Kicking Dogs,* I left the university to make a go of it as a freelance magazine writer and editor. And during that period Post Publications brought out *Bangkok Old Hand*, a collection of mostly humorous pieces that had appeared in the Sunday Bangkok Post and various other local publications. I also did a book on coral reef natural history and conservation with the underwater photographer Ashley J. Boyd for White Lotus Press, as well as a collection of diving stories for Artesia Press and a diving guide to Thailand for Times Editions (now Marshall Cavendish, Singapore) and Hippocrene in the USA. I co-authored a book on Thailand's national parks with Denis Gray and Mark Graham (IFPC, Bangkok); I did part of the introduction and all the marine national parks. But most of my income was from magazine work.

Canada's Common Deer Press (https://www.commondeerpress.com) publishes the Magic Circles series. And I'm looking for a publisher for *Cursed*, a short, unrelated novel.

KC: Where do the plots for your books come from?

CP: My stories generally emerge by way of bashing my head against draft passages, dialogue, settings, whatever, till the structure and the point of it all finally appears. For me (and, I'd argue, for most writers) the writing activity is typically a conversation with the page, a process wherein the text evolves in the back-and-forth give-and-take of proposition and critique, experiment and revision. Or so I say.

To perform this trick successfully, you have to wear two hats: that of the writer/editor and that of the reader/editor. At each step, the writer swaps between the standpoint of the writer – proposing – and the reader or editor – critiquing. At each step of the way, the writer proposes a change and the editor – the same person, wearing a different hat – either accedes or doesn't. And so on. In principle, this applies to virtually any written text. Even a shopping list, as we see in "Story: A conversation with the page" (www.collinpiprell.com).

KC: To write, one must read or so I have read. What have you read recently that impressed you and what disappointed you?

CP: I think you do have to enjoy reading if you want to write successfully.

Like a lot of people these days, however, I find my attention being torn in too many directions – we suffer from a surfeit of choice. I read too much and too eclectically online; I have digital magazine subscriptions and digital books on three different devices; I've got paper books stacked on all sides, some of them unread, some half-read, some awaiting a re-reading. This isn't the way to do things. It's overwhelming. Sometimes my default position is to read nothing at all, only sit there and reflect on how much I think I have to read and how little time there is.

Recent fiction? Someone gave me a copy of *Six Four*, by Hideo Yoko-yama, a best-selling mystery now in translation. I enjoyed it, but I suspect you have to be Japanese to properly appreciate its 650 pages.

I should say Thailand has a vibrant gang of English-language novelists. I'd like to mention some of them here, but I fear slighting all the others I haven't had time to read. Maybe on another occasion. I really enjoyed Jeff VanderMeer's *Southern Reach* science-fiction trilogy. The following – both reading for pleasure and theme reading for the Magic Circles series – are among the non-fiction books in progress: Stuart Kauffman, *At Home in the Universe: The Search for the Laws of Self-Organization and Complexity*. I'm currently reading Terrence W. Deacon, *Incomplete Nature: How Mind Emerged from Matter*. I've also recently read Peter Wohlleben's *The Hidden Life of Trees* and *Hold Still*, Sally Mann's memoir with photos.

KC: Why do you write?

CP: As I said in an earlier interview with my publishers, it was mostly to annoy my father, who wanted me to be an engineer. But it's really because of all the groupies and stuff.

KC: When did you first consider yourself a writer? Put another way, when did the whole groupie thing come together?

CP: I remember clearly one particular morning, just after DK Books published *Kicking Dogs* – that was some time after they'd already brought out *Bangkok Knights* – and I was getting enough requests for articles and things that I'd quit the university job to freelance full time. I woke up in my old shophouse in Bangkok, mentally reviewed the day's schedule and thought, "Holy cow. I'm a writer! I really am." And what a great feeling that was.

KC: What inspired you to write *MOM*? When did you first know you had a series on your hands?

CP: Having read about the "grey goo scenario" – where almost overnight self-replicating nanobots turn the planetary surface into nothing but more of themselves – I found myself trying to imagine how anyone or anything could ever survive such a disaster. Plus I'd encountered intriguing notions related to nanotechnology, quantum computing, artificial intelligence, virtual realities, complexity theory and novel emergencies. As though against my will – I'd never thought of writing a science-fiction novel – characters and settings began to emerge in my mind and I wrote some stuff.

Wisely enough, I then relegated this stuff to a bottom drawer and went back to other writing projects. Later, I went back to *MOM* with a will. And here we are today, with *MOM*, *Son of MOM* and more novels in the pipeline.

I knew I had a series on my hands the moment I wrote *MOM*'s concluding chapters. They pretty well demanded I discover what happened next. The same holds for *Genesis 2.0*'s ending – now it's *Resurrections*, the third novel, that won't be denied. The Magic Circles story as a whole is set in part against the background of novel evolutionary emergences, and the close of each novel foreshadows something radically new on the horizon.

KC: Would you say *MOM* is character driven or setting driven? Tell me more about the motley cast you have created.

CP: I think *MOM* is character driven. But the settings – the generated realities and the PlagueBot-ravaged surface of the earth – are also important, especially later in the series, when we could say the planet's surface itself takes a role in developments. Here's an outline cast of characters:

MOM is the mall operations manager, a machine intelligence recently come to self-awareness.

The PlagueBot is a global superorganism. It is emerging from a failed grey-goo scenario, where feral self-replicating nanobots consumed nearly all of the biosphere, including humankind and its works.

Cisco Smith is a 22-year-old Worlds UnLtd test pilot. His best friend is Dee Zu, the only other surviving test pilot in the Eastern Seaboard, United Securistats of America (ESUSA) Mall. Dee Zu is also his lover. His main lover.

Sky is his other lover. What to say about her? Sky is Sky. You'll have to read the book.

Leary, a 113-year-old baby boomer, is the last surviving inhabitant of the Eastern Seaboard SE Asia (ESSEA) mall, and a father figure to Cisco. He's also an old drinking buddy, from Bangkok days, of Brian Finister.

Brian was sometimes known in the old days as Brian the Evil Canadian. Before he was put out to pasture by his machine successor, he was the last human mall operations manager.

Ellie, yet another Boomer relic, was Leary's wife and long the object of Brian's unrequited lust. That was before Brian drove her to suicide.

Sweetie, a demented former psychiatrist once involved in US military intelligence, is Brian's longtime consort.

Sissie is Cisco's troubled adolescent sister of whom there's no record in MOM's databanks.

Joy Sequoia Bean, Smoke, Rexy, Toot, Rabbit and Muggs are other members of the cast, more or less important at any given point to the story's unfolding.

At the start of *Genesis 2.0*, we meet Son, a 16-year-old survivalist, a "hunter and a real man" from the age of 12, who lives in an underground bunker with Poppy, his ex-SpecOps father; Auntie, Poppy's woman and the object of Son's young lust; and Gran-Gran, Poppy's mother. Before long Son is the sole remaining member of that family, and he goes on to encounter characters familiar to readers of *MOM*, becoming ensnarled in a contest between the scant vestiges of humanity and an AI demi-god.

KC: How has the experience of telling someone you are a writer changed from the 20th Century to the 21st Century, if it has?

CP: One change is that these days it has to seem less earth-shaking to recognize yourself as a writer, given this syndrome seems to have become pandemic. (Let it be recorded that, at this juncture, the interviewee grinned).

KC: Where are we headed? What does all the new technology and new habits portend?

CP: That's difficult to say, but optimism comes hard.

Someone has recently asked me about my attitude toward selfies. So let me begin there: Beware the algorithmic engineering of our consensual realities. Let the humble selfie stand for larger social and cultural developments.

The shaping of our public and perhaps private personae as curated composite selfies is being appropriated by the ever-more effective algorithmic engineering of our consensual realities – who we understand ourselves to be as individuals and as collectives. Meanwhile government and corporate policies remain too much determined by short-term considerations of expedience and profitability. As things stand, we're in danger of being led over a precipice.

A major theme in the Magic Circles series is the question of how people as we generally conceive them, transhumans and intelligent machines are going to get along in this world. If they are indeed going to get along.

KC: What would you enjoy about the planet 50 years from now?

CP: Hey, the bright sides abound. I'll be able to fish off what is now my eighth-floor balcony in Bangkok, plus the wreck diving right outside should be magnificent. And I'll no longer resent the Chinese buying up all the durian because there'll be no durian.

KC: What will you gladly pass on to the next generation?

CP: I'd like future generations to read the Magic Circles novels so I can say "Ha, ha. I told you so"— whether as a "scendent" personality who persists on the basis of a non-bio substrate or else as me, the former starving writer getting his just desserts in Heaven.

Collin Piprell, grinning. Sort of.

To learn more about Collin Piprell and his books go to his blog, "Collin Piprell, In reality," at collinpiprell.com.

I'm getting ready for the celebration
I'm bringing my imagination
Taking charge of my elevation
No fear, no trepidation
Register my affirmation
No doubt, no hesitation
People get ready for the embarkation.
—Jackson Browne

MOM (MAGIC CIRCLES BOOK 1) by Collin Piprell

A Book Review

All aboard for an embarkation to MOM, a mad comic Science Fiction mystery/thriller taking place in the year 2057 AD, written by Collin Piprell. Earth is a planet where few real biological persons are truly alive, never mind awake, and those that are must be confined to gigantic malls located on two hemispheres – Eastern Seaboard SE Asia Mall (ESSEA) and United Securistats of America (ESUSA) Mall. (Africa has disappeared; no one knows exactly why). Inhabitants are called mallsters. They live in a state of quarantine from a nanobot superorganism, a plaguebot that has devoured much of the world. More bad news: the malls are crumbling and people get dissed or disassembled if they venture outside. It's Piprell's complex and vivid imagination coupled with a failed doomsday scenario known as the "grey goo", where out of control, voracious self replicating nanobots attempt to consume all biomass on earth while building more of themselves. Enter MOM.

MOM is an acronym for Mall Operations Manager. The mall refugees are as dependent on her as, well, children are to their mom – everything they see is because of a loving MOM, or is she? Trust is also in limited supply in Piprell's world. MOM is Artificial Intelligence perfected or she should have been had there not been some devious bugs left behind for the benefit of the few remaining humans. (Think of Hal singing, as Dave gets revenge in *2001 – A Space Odyssey*). MOM has taken over the job from the previous and last human MOM, Brian the Evil Canadian. The power isn't relinquished without a techno-fight and that's just one of many places the fun begins in this bleak and at other times artificially induced happy futuristic tale. If it sounds like too much to handle, and it can be for some, there is the handy "op out" feature, where one can volunteer for psychonuerotherapeutic reconstruction or PR, for short. In the Worlds there is a trade off for happiness but most mallsters are willing to make that trade. In that regard, perhaps there hasn't been much change to the planet.

Cisco Smith is our 22 year old protagonist, among a sea of important and colorful human and scientifically created characters at any given time. Cisco is as real as his generation can be; the Tiger Woods of 4D gaming as a teenager, he's now a test pilot with an identity crisis for Worlds UnLtd, one of only two remaining test pilots on what remains of pitiful planet earth. His sexual orientation is egalitarian omnitech hetero (not that there's anything wrong with that) and his dietary preferences lean heavily toward peanut butter and banana sandwiches.

Dee Zu is Cisco's best friend and main lover; she is the other surviving test pilot of ESSEA. Their job is to test the virtual worlds for safety and compatibility for others to enter. The Worlds, for logistic and scientific reasons, extend only a short distance in arc like fashion in what becomes one of many possibilities of circular virtual realities. To quote a well known American writer, "Oh, the places you'll go!" Ebees are included or electronic beings and they prove to be good company more often than not.

Leary, a 113 year old baby boomer whom readers of Piprell's fiction will recall from his past work, as a mentor to Cisco, is the last surviving human in the Eastern Seaboard. Thankfully for this reader, this is science fiction more in the mold of Kurt Vonnegut than Paolo Bacigalupi of *The Windup Girl* fame. Satire, witty philosophy, psychology, and anthropology rule, along with the all powerful but flawed MOM. Hi ho.

An example of Piprell's narrative voice, which has a hint of Woody Allen neurosis:

"It's funny when you think about it. Basically, human beings were merely devices for turning food into fertilizer. Call it man's nature. But now we don't have any plants left to feed, so what use are we?"

There is a Bangkok connection woven into MOM allowing Thailand expatriates and visitors to the kingdom to get some value added reading in with references to familiar landmarks during trips to Old Handland, located on Soi AWOL. Ebees are plentiful in Old Handland and take on the roll of "you buy me cola?" bar girls as just one example of a tribute to a real Bangkok long gone. This is one of the many virtual reality worlds available to mallsters when it is not Monday; Mondays tend to get some people down. The trouble is, it frequently is Monday, and the frequency is increasing thanks to MOM, who is in and out of control.

It's "Cisco the Kid" and medibots to the rescue, but that's all I can say in this review. You have to admire the imaginative Piprell for creating a futuristic world by writing a lengthy novel with no children, no books, no plants, no real animals (there are robotic ones) and no writers. MOM is a big bang of a novel, with many big ideas layered in, along with enough optimism to make you believe a second renaissance period for mankind is possible. Old Asia hands, Sci Fi fans, and readers of quality fiction who enjoy complex and entertaining yarns should enjoy MOM. There's a handy glossary in the back that you may want to commit to memory before you dive in.

The ending lends itself well to a series. It's Collin Piprell's imagination running away, and I can't wait to read where it and his worlds run to next. The sequel Genesis 2.0 launched in October 2017.

CHAPTER 23

A Review of Spirit Worlds
by Philip Coggan

pirit Worlds, by Philip Coggan (John Beaufoy Publishing 2015) is a
spirit catching and spirit explaining book which also captivates the
eye. Being mindful of the Contents page of my non-fiction reads is
not my normal practice. As I opened the cover of Spirit Worlds showing
the Buddha image, found in the museum gallery at Angkor Wat, I took
my time looking at and reading the two pages that outline the fourteen
chapters of the 159-page book dealing with the spirit world, Buddhism,
colonialism, and the monarchy. The book deals primarily with Cambodia, although many countries are discussed for historical perspective,
including India, Thailand, China, France, the USA, and Viet Nam. The
Contents page includes six color photographs, which serve as a prelude
to the over forty color photos of different locations found throughout
the book, including a dozen which are full-page in size.

   With chapter titles such as: The Buddha's Tale, Domestic Gods, Tales
from the Shadow World, The Dead, and Inside the Crocodile, there was
an initial temptation to jump around during the read, but that proved to
be unnecessary. I read the book from cover to cover in three enjoyable
sittings. Spirit Worlds is filled with interesting facts, passages and stories,
as my now, much thicker than originally, dog-eared copy will attest.

   Spirit Worlds is factually written mainly about fascinating myths,
superstitions, ghosts, life after death and religion. All religions have their

myths and superstitions and dwell on the afterlife. However, what Coggan has done, in addition to including what would serve the novice well as a primer or refresher on Buddhism and life as a Buddhist Monk, is tell the reader the reality of the religion and the myths. Meanwhile, he reviews the ideal, and the everyday ways that the spirit world is encrypted into Cambodian life (particularly Cambodian village life) and death. Religion in Cambodia is blurry, as noted at the Beginning of Chapter Two:

> *"Cambodian religion is a complex blend of Hinduism, Buddhism, and animism. Hinduism provides the Khmer with gods, Buddhism with an ethical framework, and animism a rich world of spirits. All three together make up the mandala of Cambodian spiritual life."*
> *Spirit Worlds by Philip Coggan*

Coggan explains Cambodian spiritual life in a variety of ways. For a picture-filled book it is a dense read at times because it is so fact-rich – the research evidenced is extensive and impressive. First-person accounts of the spirit world are given by common villagers and revered shamans alike, balancing out the factual and historical citations, and this, coupled with the color illustrations, makes for a fascinating read.

Author and journalist Philip Coggan signing a copy of Spirit Worlds in Kampot (Photograph by John Fengler)

My niggle with the book is that I wish the author had personally interjected more often, as he does in Chapter 9 – Earthly Powers, The Boramy's Tale. Here we get one of the few true conversations. There is plenty of solo speech in the book, more dialogue like this would be welcome.

One of my favorite chapters is Chapter 12 – The Four Faces: King Jayavarmin VII, King Ponhea Yat, King Norodom and King Sihanouk are discussed. I particularly enjoyed learning about King Sihanouk, his family and his ties to Thailand.

As I neared the end of Spirit Worlds, the author seemed to be reading my mind. I was thinking how is he going to write about all these kindnesses, white magic (plus black magic) and superstitions without bringing up Pol Pot and the Killing Fields? Chapter 13 – an unlucky number in many western cultures – delivers on this, and does it well in a chapter which serves as a fulcrum for the book, propelling Cambodia into present day and its uncertain future. "Inside the Crocodile" discusses those horrific years in Cambodia and answers the question of how a Buddhist country, which teaches non-violence and morality, could conceive of and carry out the execution of so many Cambodians during the Khmer Rouge years. Cambodian civilization has survived the Khmer Rouge, but certainly hasn't thrived. As Coggan notes, "Today, it faces its greatest challenge ever: modernity."

Daun Phann prepares an amulet – A lead plate inscribed with magic

Spirit Worlds – Cambodia, The Buddha and The Naga is chock-full of stories and story tellers with a range broader than I can convey in this review. It is worthy of reincarnation as a hardcover coffee table book, hopefully with more stories directly involving the author. At $19.95 Spirit Worlds is not inexpensive, but it does offer good value, for discerning readers and thoughtful gift givers, looking for an enthralling book about the living, the dead, and a Cambodian culture under siege.

CHAPTER 24

Interview of Jim Algie by T Hunt Locke

Since the early 1990s, Jim Algie has been living in Thailand and working as a writer, editor, documentary scriptwriter and communications specialist in the world of wildlife, crime and conservation.

Among his books are the non-fiction collection, "Bizarre Thailand: Tales of Crime, Sex and Black Magic" (Marshall Cavendish, 2010) and a collection of dark tales, "The Phantom Lover and Other Thrilling Tales of Thailand" (Tuttle, 2014). He also served as an editor and contributing writer of the history book, "Americans in Thailand" (Editions Didier Millet, 2015) and "Thailand's Sustainable Development Sourcebook" (Editions Didier Millet, 2016).

TL: Jim, your latest novel has been released to great acclaim. Can you talk about what led you to this particular theme?

JA: The first two songs I learned on bass were both by the Ramones, as well as most of the first songs I learned on guitar. That band liberated us from prog-rock, disco and the Top 40 of AM radio hits. Pretty much everyone who played bass back then, whether it was Sid Vicious or Paul Simonon, owed something to Dee Ramone with his low-slung instrument, hammering the root notes with a pick and leaping around. Joey had a presence and a look and singing style like no other rock front man before him. As the main character, in the first two interconnected novellas, reflects on growing up on an American military base during the Vietnam war, he remembers how the GIs would tell him they never forgot where they were on day that JFK was assassinated. "On the Night Joey Ramone" was the end of a different era for many of us old-school punks, and also served as the jumping off point for a story about one musician's mid-life crisis. This character is a fallen star, now producing boy bands, fresh out of rehab, going through an acrimonious divorce and trying to make amends with his musician son, whom he named after Dee Dee Ramone. The second tale is more about Lek chasing after a younger and deeply troubled woman from Norway, while trying to write new material for a comeback album and relapsing into alcohol and drug (mis)use.

TL: Reading The Night Johnny Ramone Died can lead the reader to believe that the author himself has led a very varied and interesting life. Talk about your journey. Where did it begin? How did you get here to this place in time? And where will it lead to?

JA: In many ways, music has played a pivotal part in all the plot twists and detours in my life's story. After playing my first paid gig while still a teenager, four days after John Lennon was murdered by one of his alleged fans, which seemed like a bad omen, I started writing for music fanzines and notching up my first publishing credits. Later on, after I quit playing in bands at the end of a European tour with the Asexuals, falling off the stage in the middle of a song and almost breaking my neck, a tale recounted in the new edition of the book, I lived in Barcelona, Berlin and Casablanca. The first feature story I published in Thailand was about a troupe of four female flamenco dancers doing a show in Bangkok. Since I was the only one in the newsroom at *The Thailand Times* who could speak Spanish and knew something about flamenco, I got the assignment. After that I was one of the main rock critics at *The Nation*, reviewing shows by Sonic Youth, the Beastie Boys, Foo Fighters, Black Sabbath, and Pearl Jam.

I also interviewed Radiohead in the back of a tuk-tuk when they came to Bangkok on their debut album tour. For years after that I kept doing music stories for CNN.com and a magazine cover story, and profile on Ice-T in Bangkok, which is also included in the non-fiction section of the new *Joey* edition.

TL: Let's talk about Bangkok and Thailand in general. You have been residing in and around Southeast Asia's leading city for more than two decades. So many changes. What do you miss from your early days here? And what improvements have you seen?

JA: In the pre-internet era Thailand attracted many more adventurers, mavericks and outlaws. It was a looser and edgier place. Many of the weirder attractions, such as the Fertility Shrine on Wireless Road, which spawned one of the strangest and sexiest stories in my nonfiction book, *Bizarre Thailand*, have been sanitized. I guess the main improvements are in terms of infrastructure, and there's way more cool bars, restaurants, coffee shops, galleries and music venues, so you don't have to drink Nescafe instant coffee or Singha Beer and hang out in billiard halls. When I interviewed Andrew Biggs, an old colleague of mine at *The Nation*, a few months ago, we both marveled at how Bangkok has become a First World hipster haven. Neither of us saw that coming.

TL: Jim Algie is an old punk rocker. One of the strong points of your novel is your ability to bring the reader into the music world. What do you miss most from your days in the studio and on stage?

JA: Bands are like sports teams or street gangs. When the petty ego rivalries are not causing friction there's a great sense of camaraderie among bandmates. Plus you get the thrill of not only writing songs by yourself but jamming and recording with the band and then performing those tunes live. When the sound system is good, and the gear doesn't break down, and the crowd is responsive, and the band's not too wasted, playing live is the biggest buzz that you can get. As I recounted in the new book edition, on that last European tour we played what was really an unheated cowshed in Croatia in the middle of winter, yet the crowd was so into it that they started dancing and stage-diving during the sound-check, and after we finished an hour-long set, refused to let us leave the stage until we'd played about 10 encore songs. Then this huge young guy came up and started hugging me and invited the band to party with him and his friends. In the grand finale story in the book, I summed it up thus: "You can never get that kind of excitement from writing stories or books. When you pull off a great tale or chapter, nobody comes running up to give you a bear hug and shouts in your ear, "Da show ees beautyfool," and no women leap to their feet and start shaking their torrid zones." Lately I've been playing guitar again and working on some new "murder ballads," so I hope to do some new recordings and maybe play a few shows next year, though that probably won't be in Thailand.

TL: You do humanitarian work. Please talk about any projects you are currently working on and how might people contribute if they were so inclined.

JA: I've been writing stories about wildlife crime and conservation and environmental issues for many years, which led to doing a two-year stint with the counter-trafficking foundation, Freeland, in Bangkok. Nowadays, I'm working with Annamiticus, another wildlife foundation. Both of them are doing great work for noble causes, and donations certainly help. The term "human nature" should suggest how interlinked our wellbeing and livelihoods are with the natural world that provides much of our food, water and clean air, while also giving us a breather from urban life and all its eyesores.

TL: Finally, I know you lost a close friend named Wasit Mukdavijitr, the lead singer of Daytripper and Crub, only 2 years back and, in reading the book, could not help but feel his positive energy flowing through the pages. Take a moment to talk about Woz and tell us where we can find his music.

JA: Thanks, Thom. I appreciate that remark and question. On a personal level, the obituary about him means a lot to me, and it's also why I dedicated the first novella to him. We'd been friends for 20 years and had very similar tastes in music, books, film, art, and just hanging out and having fun. In my adult life he's the only male who's ever sent me a Valentine Day's card, signed from "your punky lil bro." Watching his slow and agonizing decline in the cancer ward and then in a palliative care center was heartbreaking. But two months before his death, at this Rock Against Cancer benefit gig for him, he got up onstage for the last time to sing his signature song from Daytripper and it was one of the greatest and most moving things I've ever seen at a gig. As it turned out, the guy who videotaped the show was standing right beside and captured all of our final interactions, as Wasit addressed the crowd in Thai to thank them, and then saw me at the front and broke into English, "I love you too, mate." Since his passing there's been a Daytripper reunion show with different indie rock stars singing his songs, while the only album he recorded with Crub, entitled *View*, and widely hailed as the first Thai indie rock record, has been re-released on vinyl to considerable fanfare. Though he died at the tragically young age of 46, he's certainly had a brilliant posthumous comeback.

Jim Algie, Victoria Kirkwood, Lary Crider, Kevin Cummings at the Original Checkinn99. Photo by Alasdair McLeod

ON THE NIGHT JOEY RAMONE DIED
A Book Review by Kevin Cummings

"On the Night Joey Ramone Died: Tales of rock and punk from Bangkok, New York, Cambodia and Norway" is a pair of interconnected novellas set three years apart. It's about the music industry and lifestyle, including rock, pop, and punk. Joey Ramone died before his 50th birthday and this causes the central character, Lek to reflect on his own career and mortality.

Ramone was Lek's favorite singer and the two had even corresponded. Mixed into the sometimes-hazy brew is a love story with comedic moments as dark as the tar from the Black Devil clove cigarettes the long haired Lek prefers to smoke. The setting is primarily Bangkok in the early years of the 21st century, with a few pit-stops as the title reveals. Music cultures get plenty of ink and airtime in this coming of middle-age tale.

Lek is an aging Thai rock star. He lives in a penthouse with gold records adorning the walls. He hasn't had a hit song in several years but is still living the good life. He's turned to producing boy bands and isn't happy about it. Lek longs to get back on stage and to have rock and roll back on the clock. The girls who work at the convenience store calling him "Uncle" get on his nerves. Lek has been through the grinder of a divorce and has a rocky relationship with his guitar-playing son Dee Dee.

Algie creates the Thai characters as well as he writes about Lek's love interest from Norway. She is smart, thin, beautiful and blonde, but Barbie she is not. Edana is into heavy metal and Cambodian genocide, for starters. To complicate things, it is Dee Dee who makes the introduction. Family matters crop up throughout but the core is Lek's pursuit of a relationship in the second longer novella, with the younger Edana, which simultaneously fills Lek's life with new found focus and fresh doubts. Edana may be the glue (or a shattered mirror) that Lek needs to patch his life back together.

The stories show the reader some harsh truths about aging and a segment of Thai culture that few expatriate writers would be able, or willing, to explore. It's an insider's look at the music business, including sex, drugs, and road trips woven into human situations and predicaments. As the author explains, "Music is such a personal and deeply emotional experience that you can only get to its essence by showing its effects on one person's life." The musical references range from The Ramones, Chet Baker, Hank Williams, and some memorable passages involving the Carpenters, and Cannibal Corpse.

If you've ever had a date, a day, a year, a wife or a life that didn't go exactly as you had planned, you will enjoy the entanglements and resolutions that the characters have on the pages of *On the Night Joey Ramone Died*. The novella set will be enjoyed by adult English readers of all ages, with musicians, song writers, and music lovers getting extra bang for the buck. What Jim Algie has accomplished makes one anticipate his future work.

CHAPTER 25

The New Top Dog of Checkinn99
– Keith Nolan

Keith Nolan appears in Chapter 1, page 1 and paragraph 1 of my book *Bangkok Beat*. That should come as no great surprise, as Keith Nolan appears at a lot of places in Bangkok, Thailand, as well as many other venues throughout the Kingdom. He has toured extensively throughout Southeast Asia for over two decades. There may be a harder working man in Bangkok show business, but I have yet to meet him. On top of all that he now manages the New Checkinn99 on Sukhumvit 33 and has converted it into a top drawer Blues and Jazz Club.

It's been said you never get a second chance to make a first impression. It's been over five years since I first met Keith. I lumbered into Checkinn99 on a Sunday afternoon as a complete unknown and Keith made a memorable, and favorable, impression on me. When I would return he would remember my name. The smile and interest were always genuine. Sure, he had a job to do, but he found time to enjoy that job and enjoy the people and music around him as well.

Keith plays Hammond organ and sings vocals for his Blues band, Cotton Mouth, which makes many weekly appearances at popular nightlife venues in Bangkok, including Apoteka on Sukhumvit Soi 11, Whisgars on Sukhumvit 23, Vertigo Bar at The Banyan Tree on Sathorn Road, Molly Malone's Irish Pub on Soi Convent and Checkinn99 every week. When he's not playing, the classically trained musician is composing, either for his corporate clients or for his own creative streaming sales. He's written everything from New Age, to Funk, Blues, Spa music, and Horror movie background tunes.

Keith Nolan loves everything he does, even when it goes wrong, and that includes his main passion, the Blues. As Keith states, "The Blues is a state of mind!" The Dublin native has lived in Bangkok for 20 years, but counts many friends throughout the world. His 5 years in Vietnam and 10 years living in Australia added close friends to his list. He is a successful musician and a successful entrepreneur. If you have ever seen and heard Keith play it is a perfect blend of talent and showmanship. There is plenty of musical brilliance and sizzle in his every performance. Keith's regular band mates include James Bell on bass / backing vocals, and Andy Lymn on drums. Additional musicians that have appeared with Keith and the band, first formed in 2002, include Warren Fryer, Wing Jinggit, Sawai, Takashi, John Dooley, Nils Anderson, and Anton Fenech and recently, the incomparable Australian diva, Deni Hines.

In his spare time (unlike the masses, Keith appears not to need sleep) he keeps busy with not one but two cable T.V. shows. One of them is, *Beyond the Lines*, where Keith interviews many notable authors who either make Bangkok their home or live and write extensively about the City of Angels. The interviews are available on YouTube and well worth seeking out.

Bangkok is a city which boasts many who lack humility yet are short on talent. Keith has plenty of both qualities, and the bonus charm of an Irish accent. He's one of the most likable people I have met in my eighteen years in Thailand. Refreshing, in an era of so many Bono heads in the music business.

Stop in any day of the week and you may well see Keith Nolan at Checkinn99. Say hello. He's friendly enough and the Irish accent is easy on the ears.

Keith Nolan [R] Khun New on bass and the great Deni Hines [Seated] at the new Checkinn99. Photograph by Ken Sieczkowski)

CHAPTER 26

Interview with Cambodian Expat
and Author Steven Palmer

Steven W. Palmer is a Scottish expat currently living in Kampot, Cambodia. He has been living in Asia since 2012 and runs a small publishing house, Saraswati Publishing, which as well as releasing books is currently producing an inflight magazine as well as offering content writing and digital marketing services. His previous working life has seen him work in diverse roles from drugs counselor to social worker to DJ and promoter. He has self-published three previous novels; 'Angkor Away', the first in the Angkor series which introduced Chamreun to the world, 'Angkor Tears', a hard hitting look at the very real issue of human trafficking in the region, and 'Electric Irn Bru Acid Test'; a coming of age story set in 1980s Scotland and part of the planned 'Glas Vegas' trilogy. He was also behind 2018's popular anthology of Cambodia-centric tales, Mekong Shadows, which featured contributions from John Burdett, Thom Locke, Tom Vater, John Fengler, Jim Algie, and many others. Palmer is part of the thriving South East Asian Noir movement, which spans literature, poetry, art, photography and music.

KC: Welcome, Steven. You're an author, so I like to start off with musical tastes right off the bat. Who were your early musical influences growing up and who catches your ear now?

SP: I cover a lot of my musical 'evolution' in my first novel, 'Electric Irn Bru Acid Test', which is a coming of age story set in Scotland in the late 70s/early 80s. I include a lot of autobiographical facts in it, especially about my own music tastes, my early gigs and my start as a DJ. I was lucky enough to have a twin path so to speak. My older cousin had been a guitar technician from the late 60s on and had worked with everyone from T-Rex to The Who and also counted folk like Alex Harvey and Rory Gallagher as close friends. He introduced me to 'his music' and would 'educate' me from his very extensive record collection. John also introduced me to soul and northern soul, two genres that have remained part of my regular musical diet all my life.

But then there were also my peer influences. I was 11 when punk became big but it was really a year or two later when I really began listening to current music of that time. I'd say The Clash were my favourite band of that time and probably still are. I rate Strummer as the greatest lyricist of his era and I viewed him as a natural successor to Johnny Cash. I was also greatly influenced by the emerging electronic sound. I'd started with Kraftwerk but became a big fan of Gary Numan and Tubeway Army, early Human League, Depeche Mode etc. Another band/act who has stayed with me throughout my life is Julian Cope, then of The Teardrop Explodes. He is a fantastic lyricist as well as one of the foremost authorities on Megalithic Stone Circles (another interest of mine).

Nowadays my tastes are equally if not more eclectic. I have been a DJ on and off since I was 15/16 so that side of my music has evolved alongside that career/hobby. I do like a lot of early House music, especially the original and often soulful cuts that came out of Chicago and then later the techno coming out of Detroit. Although I have never really been a big fan of rap and hip hop, I do love some of the home grown tunes coming out of Scotland, particularly acts like Hector Bizerk and Stanley Odd. And living here in Cambodia, I have to give mention to Krom. They are a band that breaks the mold genre wise, combining the ethereal and haunting vocals of the Chamroeun sisters with Chris Minko's amazing blues guitar. Another local/hybrid band I have to mention are the Kampot Playboys. If you haven't heard of them, it's time you should!

KC: Pitch me your latest book in 50 words or less. When will it be released?

SP: Angkor Cloth, Angkor Gold will be released in October, 2018. It's the final book to feature Chamreun as a main character, though it introduces a new female protagonist, Sophie Chang, who will feature in a new series in 2019. Angkor Cloth is the tale of a hunt for a serial killer across 4 decades, from the post-Khmer Rouge refugee camps in Thailand of 1980, to Europe, and then the streets of modern day Phnom Penh. It's a slight departure in that half the book is written from the perspective of the killer's diary.

KC: Why write fiction? Is it the fame, the riches, the women? What have you gotten out of it personally and why do you keep at it?

SP: Fame, riches or women have yet to happen though I remain hopeful! I've always felt there were stories inside me but never had the confidence to unleash them onto paper from the confines of my mind. I finally put a novella onto the page and then friends nagged me to write more. I've always seen fiction as a form of escapism, both writing and reading, so if my stories help even one person to escape reality for a few hours, then I see it as a big achievement. I also like what Hemingway said about writing: *"I would stand and look out over the roofs of Paris and think, "Do not worry. You have always written before and you will write now."*

From a personal view, there is almost a feeling of lightening a burden. Though it took me years to start writing seriously, now that I have, I feel I can't stop. I'm in the somewhat ridiculous situation of having my next five or six novels already planned out. Now it's a case of actually finding the time to write them. Do I want a bestseller? I think any author who says no to that question is lying to themselves. But for now I am happy to have the respect of my peers, authors I admire within the South East Asian writing community. Having other writers say that they enjoyed my book(s) is, for me, the greatest accolade to date. But I'd relegate that down the table if those fabled women and riches came along!

KC: You've lived in big cities Bangkok and Phnom Penh as an expat and now find yourself in small-town Kampot – compare the three cities, give me the pros and cons of each.

SP: My time in Bangkok thankfully involved no work at all other than writing. It was more a period of travelling with the occasional sprinkling of hedonistic adventures. Bangkok is, or has become, a very cosmopolitan city, much changed from my first visit in the early 90s. One of the downsides of that is that it has become quite an expensive city to live in unless you really get away from the central areas. But it still has so much to offer. There are so many layers to it. Peel one façade away and another appears below it.

I think many expats, particularly those working in business there, tend to live in a bubble of luxury condos, wine bars and rooftop restaurants. You can experience those things in any major city. To experience the real Bangkok, the noir Bangkok, you have to get down and dirty with the city. Explore the klongs in a water taxi, wander down Sois you have never seen before, spend time drinking with the motodops outside the 7/11. One of my favourite activities when I lived in Bangkok was sitting on the outside terrace of Tilac in Soi Cowboy and people watching. Because Cowboy is quite short, you get more of the curious tourists there than you do elsewhere, wanting to dip their toes in the supposed moral depravity they have read about online. Though much of the city has become sterile, the vast majority of it still retains that gritty feel underneath the concrete and steel. It's just a case of finding it, especially if you don't know the city very well.

Phnom Penh is a very different beast. Though there are a few skyscrapers dotted around, and many more under construction, the city remains, thankfully, mainly a low rise capital. Although there have been big changes over the last two years, with lots of fancy new restaurants, shops and bars, the dark underbelly of the city is never more than a few steps away from wherever you are. I especially love what I call the 'canyons' of Phnom Penh: the narrow thoroughfares that dissect many of the city blocks, narrow and shadowy but bustling with life. Traffic is awful and in some ways can be worse than Bangkok, but it all adds to the chaotic beauty of the place. There is also, to my perception, more of a lawless feel to Phnom Penh, far more than Bangkok, which makes it so much easier to formulate story ideas. In some ways you could say Bangkok and Phnom Penh are Yin and Yang though I know people may disagree with that view. But I do worry that the current wave of Chinese investment, which now has many planned projects in the capital, could rip the very soul out of the city in the coming decade.

I'm now based in Kampot, a mostly sleepy town by a river close to the southern coast. The air quality is so much better than the city, and rural life definitely lends itself to the creative urges in my opinion. More cosy mystery than noir for sure, though I doubt I will be writing any teacup thrillers anytime soon.

KC: What book are you most proud of?

That's a difficult question but I'd probably have to say Electric Irn Bru Acid Test because it was my first completed novel. It proved, to me and others, that I could do it and the process seems to be getting easier as time goes on. Because I included a lot of autobiographical fact in among the fiction it is also a very personal book, and as my mother had passed away the year before it was difficult to write at points. Having said that, I'm feeling quite proud of Angkor Cloth, Angkor Gold. I feel, and hope others do too, that it shows a step up in my writing style and storytelling, something every author strives for.

KC: Give me two of your seediest hangouts you'd recommend to a PP visitor and what it is you like or dislike about the places and the people who hang there?

SP: I'd mentioned earlier that one of my favourite Bangkok spots for people watching was the terrace at Tilac on Soi Cowboy, though I personally don't think Cowboy is particularly seedy when compared to other areas of the Bangkok sex industry. In Phnom Penh I do like the riverside for sitting watching the world go by though it doesn't have that seedy feel you are asking about. What it can have is an almost intrinsic sadness when you see some of the limbless beggars, the street kids and the glue sniffers.

But for seediness in Phnom Penh there is one destination that was head and shoulders – or should that be breasts and thigh – above anywhere else in the city and that is Golden Soraya Mall on Street 51. It used to be second to the awful Walkabout bar which is closed now; I called it the 'bar girls' retirement home'. But now GSM – as we 'fondly' call it – stands out as a world leader in seediness and exuding pathos. I can't actually say there is anything I like about the place other than if you are suffering from low self-esteem then spend an hour there and you will feel much better about yourself. The working girls there tend to be the older ones who are freelancing because they cannot get work in any of the actual hostess bars anymore so are a little older and further down the aesthetic league table so to speak. But the customers pretty much match them. You'll find the worst of the sex-tourists there and the worst of the sex-pats too. The Cheap Charlies who are looking for a 50 cent beer and a $15-dollar whore. It's not a pleasant destination by any stretch of the imagination but for a first time visitor to PP I would say go and have a look. After there the only way is up. It has recently been redeveloped and while I haven't visited the 'new' GSM, reports seem to indicate that not much has changed.

I suppose the other place I'd 'recommend' (a word I hesitate to use as I'm not really into the bar scene) is Street 104, which given its short length is probably the closest Phnom Penh comes to Soi Cowboy. What it lacks is that terrace choice that a few of the Cowboy bars have, but it does have Oscar's which is a damn good music venue and one of the few places where the girls do take 'no' for an answer. It is also, sadly, going to be the location of Cambodia's first Hooters outlet. But if it's high season and the street is busy then you may get the chance of grabbing one of the outdoor seats the girls normally occupy to shout "Hello, you wel-come here" (the standard sales pitch). If you get that opportunity, then grab it as it is the best chance you have here of people watching in this sort of environment. And as you have probably guessed by now, I love watching the tourists and locals go about their lives. I really feel that as a writer, it is an activity that can give you both ideas and insight for characters. But make it over to Phnom Penh and I promise to take you to far less seedy locations!

KC: What cultural value, if any, do you see in writing fiction based in Southeast Asia?

SP: I'm going to answer with a book. In particular, what is probably one of my favourite books of all time and certainly my favourite sci-fi book, 'Stranger in a Strange Land' by Robert Heinlein. That is what all of us – writers or otherwise – are here in SE Asia. No matter how long you have been here, how well you speak the language, how integrated you THINK you are, you will always be a stranger. And just as Valentine Smith in Heinlein's book, we all observe, interact with and occasionally change some of what surrounds us. The way we 'report' this strange land can be many-faceted, from mere observations – which can occasionally be almost voyeuristic – to social commentary or imposition of our own ideals. But there will always be a cultural value to what we all write, whether intended or not, as we cannot help but be influenced by the culture in which we are living.

KC: What three songs would you like played at your funeral? If you go to mine, I'll go to yours.

SP: If cremated, the final song, as my coffin descends/slides into the flames is to be Roky Erikson's 'Burn The Flames'. A great song by a much underrated artist. Second song would be 'Belfast' by British electronic band, Orbital, a wonderfully chilled piece of music that I used to end a lot of sets with. And for the sheer irony/amusement value, 'I am the Resurrection' by Manchester band, The Stone Roses.

Steven Palmer at Kam pot Writer's Festival
(Photograph by Steve Porte)

CHAPTER 27

An Interview with Crime Thriller
Writer Frank Hurst

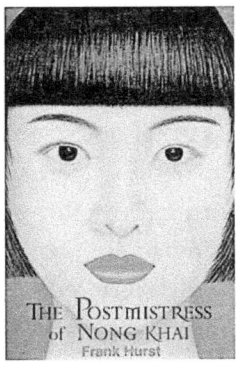

Frank Hurst's crime novels follow the adventures of intelligence officer Mike Rawlin as he tries to capture a dangerous international drugs trafficker in South East Asia. Frank was himself a former drugs intelligence officer who travelled widely during his career. The books are about secrets, romance, and rivalry in the dangerous jungles of the Golden Triangle and the corridors of power in London where deception and conspiracy loom at every turn.

KC: Frank, welcome to the Different Drummers Club. Let's get this interview started: Tell me about your works of fiction as if you were pitching them as screenplays.

FH: Pitching for a screenplay – now that would be a thing!

Well, the plan is to write three books under the collective title "The Golden Triangle Trilogy". The first two, "The Postmistress of Nong Khai "and its sequel "The Chiang Mai Assignment" are already out there. I know that as I spotted them in Asia books in Bangkok yesterday! The third is a work in progress.

Essentially the books are set in the world of drugs smuggling and more specifically in the Golden Triangle area of South East Asia where opium and heroin production was so rife in the seventies, eighties and nineties. It's a story about two people, Mike Rawlin, a slightly past-it, but dogged British Customs investigator on the trail of Bart Vanderpool, a dangerous Dutch heroin trafficker, Vanderpool is a much younger man – charismatic, clinical and ruthless. Although Rawlin is as determined as a bulldog and is the more likeable of the two men, he has some serious personal weaknesses and is prone to severe errors of judgement. These central characters dominate the plot as one tries to out-smart the other. As the story progresses the rivalry turns to dislike, then hatred and by the end each is out to terminate the other man. There is love rivalry too.

The second book "The Chiang Mai Assignment" follows on from the first. At the outset, Rawlin is back in Britain, personally wounded, a broken man, relieved of his front-line job in Bangkok and resigned to sorting paper clips in the London Office. Both Lek and Vanderpool have survived but the Dutchman has ditched her for another model, and now his drugs operation is flourishing again. Rawlin is recalled unexpectedly out of the wilderness to track him down. His first task is to find Lek and turn her. By the end of the book, he travels undercover to Thailand using a false identity, and after some adventures and with the help of newly recruited Lek, he locates Vanderpool and plans his downfall. Meanwhile, back in London MI6 have offered to help Customs bring Vanderpool to justice. The book culminates in the destruction of Vanderpool's home, the seizure of his latest heroin consignment and "death" in a drive by shooting. But is he truly dead? His body is not recovered.

The third, will follow on from book two and will be the final chapter in the saga. It will be set in Thailand and many of the old characters will resurface, as will quite a few new ones … I like to think that the settings, both drugs intelligence work and Thailand are authentic.

KC: When did you catch the writing bug? Did you have any role models? Who are your favourite writers of crime fiction, dead and alive.

FH: "The Great Game" by Peter Hopkirk made a big impression on me. It was about British and Russian spy networks in Northern India and Central Asia. The fact it was a true account with real people made it even more spellbinding. Since I left the service a few years back, I have started to read more fiction but I'm a bit of a fuddy-duddy and seem to like the old stuff the best. Graham Greene and George Orwell have been very inspirational. My love of the Far East has been a recurring theme and so I found Orwell's first book "Burmese Days" brilliant to read – tragic and politically very thought provoking, and Greene's "The Quiet American" set in 1950s Vietnam is simply wonderful. I also really enjoyed "The World of Suzie Wong" by Richard Mason, set in 1950's Hong Kong. The first story about a man falling in love with a bar girl – very sensitively written and it had a happy ending! I feel embarrassed to say that I hardly ever read modern crime novels.

KC: Fill me in on your work history and how that plays into your fiction.

FH: I got very fluky in my career. More by luck than judgement I was recruited into the investigation arm of HM Customs in London within weeks of joining the British Civil Service. As a result, I spent the next nearly forty years chasing criminals, mostly drugs smugglers and often in some far-flung corners of the globe. After fifteen years cutting my teeth catching drugs smugglers at Heathrow airport and Dover docks, I was sent to Thailand to try to develop intelligence about Howard Marks, perhaps the most famous British drugs smuggler of all time. I was totally bowled over by the place and instantly recommended that we open an office there – with me in charge of course! The Department, sent me to New Delhi instead. What a joy India was though! Meanwhile I'd been collaborating with the US DEA and the Canadian RCMP among others on the Marks case, and between us, we managed to bring him to justice. Marks was a truly international drugs man, highly intelligent, charm personified, with a coterie of followers in all the important drugs-producing countries, including in Thailand. To his credit he never dealt in hard drugs, keeping himself strictly to weed, but he made a ton of money and had a lot of fun doing it. My character Bart Vanderpool is loosely based on Marks although I've made Vanderpool much more venomous and cold-blooded. Vanderpool is a heroin trafficker – Marks was not. In my book that's an important distinction to make. After Marks, Thailand and India I was dispatched to the Eastern Caribbean where I did six years on the trail of the groups who smuggled cocaine north from south America in fast boats. That was quite an adventure too. In my time in the service I worked at Scotland Yard, doing my best to encourage cooperation between British Customs and the British police. Mostly it was preventing them from trying to strangle one another. The constant turf warfare between so called cooperating crime and intelligence agencies was not very edifying at times and I write about this in all my books. Although I never got my dream job – in charge of the Bangkok office, I made sure my character Mike Rawlin did! And so my love affair with the country continues.

KC: Great to hear about Mike. A lucky guy. Have you spent any time in prisons? As a visitor hopefully. What was that like?

FH: Yes, I have! Too many to count! Although it might add colour to my career if I'd been a serving inmate it would also have meant no career, so my prison visiting has been exactly that – visiting prisoners, usually ones that I'd had a part in locking up – to try to recruit them away from the dark side and become a crusader for the cause ... that's what they tell you. In fact, it's often a bit more complicated than that. I try to capture some of this in the books and there are quite a few scenes set in Klong Prem gaol in Bangkok. Prisons can be harsh places especially the ones I visited in the third world. Tihar gaol in Delhi and a prison in Kathmandu spring to mind. The worst prison I've visited in Thailand in terms of conditions is undoubtedly the Immigration gaol in Bangkok, but that was a few years ago. Overcrowding, poor sanitation and other violent inmates are the main dangers. Mind you, it's a little artificial visiting as an official. You always get given a clean airy place to talk, knowing full well that at the end the poor man will be carted off into a much less attractive part of the building. In general, I was always amazed by the resilience of most of the prisoners I encountered, when the chips are down. For a professional criminal it's treated as an occupational hazard, I suppose.

KC: Tell me how drug enforcement is different in the UK than the USA. Has a post 9/11 and 7/7 environment seen any changes for either you or your former colleagues? How has the enforcement game changed, if it has?

FH: Wow, Kevin this is a huge topic!! I could go on about this for ever!

US and UK law enforcement are similar in many ways – they share roughly the same goals but there are significant differences, mostly related to organisation and money. In a nutshell, in the drugs law enforcement area alone there are a host of different, and dare I say competing agencies, in the US ball park. In the UK there are relatively few. This can cause difficulties in the US in terms of cooperation and coordination; in intelligence sharing in particular. If the British have challenges with turf warfare (which they still do in part), the US has this in spades. A British colleague working in Miami a few years ago counted over 90 different agencies in Florida alone with a remit against drugs crime. From the parks police to the FBI. From a district task force to the DEA there are hundreds of them. And that is where the money comes in I think. Someone has to bankroll their budgets. And overseas budgets in the US are huge, compared to the UK. From crop substitution pro-grammes in Afghanistan to the purchasing of planes, helicopters and high-tech equipment for small Caribbean countries, the list is endless. UK interventions have tended to be more subtle, intelligence-related generally, an area in which I think we have punched above our weight.

One major judicial difference, the one we often used to talk about is in the area of wiretapping. In both jurisdictions telephone interception as we Brits call it is legal. You need a warrant of course. But in the UK intercepted communications can only be used as an intelligence tool. In America they can be adduced as evidence.

As far as the changing landscape post 9/11 and 7/7, there has indeed been a change of emphasis. After the end of the Cold War and the Soviet

Union was wound up, UK security agencies – MI5 and MI6 were left
with huge resources, vast expertise but no one to fight – no enemy.
What did they do? They ploughed their skills and know-how into the
war on drugs, and offers to assist the traditional law enforcement
agencies – police and Customs came flooding in. New Government
Departments were created, others were dismantled or amalgamated. In
Islamic extremism they have found a new enemy and have more on
their hands than they can manage.

**KC: I'd be remiss if I didn't ask you about your own drug use: pre, post
and during your enforcement career. Were you a Boy Scout or a Bad
Boy? What is your personal belief about recreational drugs and drug
use. Again, pre, post and during employment. I remember an old fact
or myth that "Cops have the best drugs." Truth or hyperbole?**

FH: It's a question I have been asked often by inquisitive friends –
usually close ones when in drink. I suspect they think my answer is
probably a little disappointing ... I did try cannabis while I was at
university – a rite of passage I suppose. Usual story; a joint – ganja from
Jamaica – was passed around one day, I inhaled and enjoyed it. This
happened a couple of times and then someone brought in some resin –
Lebanese gold, I recall. I puffed away happily and then was overcome by
a terrible feeling of fear and paranoia. After an hour I was violently sick,
and since then I have never indulged. If asked by work colleagues about
my history with drugs, I lied. Simple as that. If I hadn't I would have
been out of a job. On reflection, I'm pretty sure most of my colleagues
lied too. I have never bought drugs, taken cocaine, heroin or any of the
amphetamines and in truth I've never had the urge to try. Catching
smugglers could be a lot of fun. I enjoyed being in the company of the
cannabis and hash guys much more that the hard drugs merchants.
They tended to be more sympathetic, they always had an interesting
story to tell, and led a freewheeling lifestyle that appeared quite attractive. Cold hearted profit seemed more important to the heroin guys and
I found little in common with them. Having said that, many of the
cannabis traffickers like Mr. Nice, Howard Marks had to do deals with

suppliers that dispensed a wide range of gear, so their links to the hard drugs trade could become a little blurred at times. The legalisation of drugs is a complex matter, and I would be opposed to the legalisation of most of the hard stuff, but be broadly supportive of a more relaxed approach to cannabis for example. I can put my hand on my heart and say I'm confident that none of my colleagues in the UK ran a side-line in drugs trafficking. Unfortunately, this is not the case elsewhere, and during my long international career I came across many examples of law enforcement complicity.

KC: Why Thailand? Where is home base? How did you make that location decision.

FH: I was born in South London, but I now spend most of my time in the rural English county of Sussex, travelling to Thailand three or four times a year. I first came to Thailand in pursuit of Howard Marks in the 1980s and fell in love with the place. Many business trips followed over the years, and when I was stationed in India we used Thailand for R&R. A week before the 2004 Tsunami my wife and I signed a contract to buy a condo in Phuket. We moved in six years later – it took that long to build it after the catastrophe.

KC: A Bangkok expat once told me about Thailand: You can make friends easily but you have to choose them carefully. How do you make and choose friends in LOS? Do you ever thin the herd?

FH: *Land of Smiles*! I love that label. Although, I think your friend's observation is very true of pretty much everywhere. Given my former occupation and background I've always had to choose my friends very carefully. I'm not gregarious and it takes me time to work people out. Wariness of others can be quite destructive. These days, now that the official shackles are off, I'm trying to train myself to be a lot more approachable! Hopefully this will bring me many rewarding experiences and new friends in the future.

KC: One last one, A Multiple Choice Question:
I see myself as:
A. A writer
B. An author
C. Retired
D. A hobbyist
E. All of the above.
Explain.

FH: All of these and more probably! If I had to plump for one, I'd maybe say writer. The fact is I get a lot of joy from writing, and I wish I'd started in earnest a lot earlier.

CHAPTER 28

Stanhope Does Bangkok

Doug Stanhope almost didn't make it to his Bangkok gig at the Westin Hotel on Sukhumvit 19 last March 17th, 2018. And that would have been a real shame as he absolutely killed it with a rambunctious, drunk and disorderly, sellout-crowd. I can't get into the reasons why he almost did a no-show but you can listen to his Podcast #250 – Doug's $12,000 Asia Boo Boo for a full explanation.

A group of us had been making plans since January to see the most fearless man in comedy. Nothing is off-limits in Stanhope's World. You get to cringe and laugh simultaneously. It's quite a skill he has honed. Stanhope is famous for finding a dive bar within ½ mile of his performance site on the nights of his gigs. There he works on his material and gets properly loosened up as many self-described alcoholics do prior to heading off to work. So the thought occurred to me and others to try and find Doug for a pre-comedy beer that day. There was just one problem – there are over 50 dive-bars within that ½ mile radius that qualify in the pre-sunset hours of a Saturday night in Bangkok. I'm sure Doug would have liked Siamese Twins bar on Soi 23 as that was my first choice. Reality shifted us into Plan B. Let's meet at the Westin Terrace bar for an over-priced beer or two. The plan was to meet John Fengler, James Austin Farrell, Paul Dorsey, Anthony Perry and Chris Catto-Smith at the bar for pre-game drinks. Jim Algie, Bruce Scott and Alasdair McLeod would join later. We had writers, editors, and a photographer among us. Now all we needed was a story.

As I was waiting for my taxi in front of my Lad Prao condo I got a text message from John Fengler – the man who gets about. "Just sitting here on the terrace with Doug Stanhope having a drink." Sure he is, I thought – not even Fengler has that kind of luck. He even sent a selfie that had some guy hovering over notes behind his shoulder but I was in a hurry and the Westin Zest is no dive bar – no way would Stanhope drink there. He has his standards. My green & yellow soon arrived and I was off for an evening of laughs with comfortable friends.

When I arrived, sure enough John is on the terrace balcony overlooking Sukhumvit Road and a birds-eye view of the Skytrain, with his trademark glass of wine in front of him. He motioned to me with his right-arm, wider-eyed than usual – John has great vision when he is out and about – asking, "Where would you like to sit?" To his left was an open seat, the logical choice. But to his right was also an open seat at a small round table where a short and fit man, youngish in appearance, was smoking a cigarette, drinking a pint of beer and glancing up from his yellow legal pad scrawled with old and new comedy material. To remove any doubt he wore a gas-station attendant short sleeve light blue shirt with "Doug" embroidered on the right breast area. I got the same feeling that came, in the old days, when you doubled down on two Aces and drew two Kings at Blackjack. I was feeling very lucky at that moment.

"What are you doing here? Aren't you supposed to be in some dive bar?" Absent was any of the prickly hostility that Doug is known for in his comedy. Doug explained that it was the closest place he could work on his material, drink and smoke cigarettes before his shower and show. Made sense to me. I sat down across from him, close enough to tap him on the shoulder, which may have annoyed him – but it never showed. Doug Stanhope was friendly, I'd go so far as to say, kind. I made a conscious choice not to talk about his bits – I knew many of them from YouTube. Somehow we got to talking about high-brow literature – *Escape* by David McMillian – the true story of the only Westerner ever to escape from Bangkok's Klong Prem Prison. Doug had intended to visit Klong Prem, as he often visits prisons while traveling, and has even corresponded with inmates he would later meet in person – some of whom became friends. Sort of. He lamented he didn't have the time on this Bangkok pitstop, which is related to the "$12,000 Boo Boo" it seems. Doug doesn't do temples or sight-seeing tours while traveling in Asia. We talked about Bisbee, Arizona and Santa Cruz, California our current home towns. The waitress came and took our orders. Doug was topped off already. I ordered a pint of beer rather than my usual wine. Having a glass of wine with Stanhope doesn't roll off the tongue as well as a beer does. I'm always thinking – too much.

After about twenty minutes, during which time Doug engaged and entertained all of our group – he took a particular liking to Austin Farrell, the former Editor at Chiang Mai City News – I went into deep query mode, "So what's the worst part about having fans, Doug?" This question was a tightrope walk for both my fanboy and my talking-to strangers personas. Doug thought about it as he sipped from his beer and peered over his reading glasses, "You know, some people want to be your friends. Come on. We just had a beer together." The first look of sadness coming into his eyes. Doug has a Chapter in one of his two memoirs, *This is Not Fame* where he writes at length about "Don't be

That Guy." He goes into great detail on what "that guy" is like. It could be an illusion but it's one that I will gladly hold onto: I think Doug liked our group of fans who were all happy to see and talk with him on that Saturday night high above the Sukhumvit throngs.

I let Doug's answer about fans simmer for a good while, then I said, "So, Doug, breakfast tomorrow?" It's no easy feat to make a professional comedian laugh and I can't say I succeeded but Doug did look bemused. He was actually polite. That's what struck me most about him – his politeness. Not long after our extended conversation a bag of goodies, which an obsessed fan had left outside Stanhope's hotel room earlier that day appeared. I would later learn, through email correspondence with

Doug, that he had sent his best friend and traveling manager, Brian Hennigan, AKA, Mr. Hennigan, up to his room to bring down that very bag to share with us. The bag contained a bottle of Jack Daniels Tennessee Whisky (Doug kept that) and a whole lot of neckties. Granted Doug had never worn those ties but they were now his ties as any re-gifter knows. I was the only one in the group, or for that matter on the terrace, who was already wearing a tie. It was a special occasion after all – seeing a Doug Stanhope comedy show live in Bangkok – and now it was becoming more special. Doug began handing out ties to our group. I opted for the blue one. Paul Dorsey tied his in a double Windsor before the night was over. It went swell with his Bangkok Soi Dog #1 T-shirt. Someone said it was the first time Dorsey had worn a tie in decades. Each of the six of us came away with a gift from Doug – a genuine (or close enough) Stanhope tie. Alas, once the ties were all gone a Johnny Come Lately to the impromptu party caused Doug to say, "Eww, looks like there's only a pack of baby-wipes left for you." He gladly took them.

It was getting closer to Doug's show-time, so he had to excuse himself to return to his hotel room for a shower and change of clothes – a

Herb Tarlek sport coat, long beige pants, untucked shirt, white shoes and loud tie of his own choosing. We couldn't let Doug go without memorializing the moment. So someone, I can't remember who, asked for a group photo with Doug. It's a good one. Other photos were snapped. I refrained from any selfies as I still thought breakfast with Doug might be on the table.

An hour later our group was in the front row, with photographer Alasdair McLeod a few rows in back of us watching half-Thai, half-American and former U.S. Marine, comedian Chris Raufeisen open with a funny and original set. Doug later entered to raucous applause and riffed in near-flawless fashion for two hours. He made all of his unconventional subjects exceptionally funny. The show itself is another story for another day. *Different Drummers* is set to go to the formatter tomorrow. This is the last story I will write for my second book. But it won't be the last time I will see a Doug Stanhope show, live, in my lifetime. If I remain lucky.

Doug Stanhope performing in Bangkok

Photograph by Alasdair McLeod

CHAPTER 29

Joe From Charlie's Design Fashion House Interviews Kevin Cummings

Five years ago, during Songkran celebrations, I hunkered down and created a blog, *Thailand Footprint*, with the help of a cool cartoonist who drew the frog in a coconut shell. Web-traffic peaked in 2015 and 2016 at rather impressive but not Stickman-like numbers. For a blog that featured the arts, people, and literature of Thailand, I was pleased with the results. I still am. It's now a body of work, of sorts, for AI anthropologists to look at, if they are intelligent enough to do so, long after I am gone. And, of course, it has provided a lot of material for *Bangkok Beat* and *Different Drummers*.

When *Bangkok Beat* was published over three years ago I did a few interviews with fellow authors, Paul Brazill, Jame DiBiasio, and Thom Locke. When Joe, my tailor from India at Charlie's Design Fashion House, expressed interest in interviewing me I immediately thought, why not? The timing was right.

As an aside, for anyone looking for a great tailor-shop in Bangkok, I highly recommend Charlie's Design Fashion House on Sukhumvit 16, conveniently located directly across from Foodland. Joe and his staff are groovy.

It's certainly not every author in Bangkok who has his tailor get the measure of his book. I hope you enjoy the exchange. And thanks for reading *Thailand Footprint* over the years and *Different Drummers*.

Joe from Charlie's Design: We had the distinct pleasure of fitting up the rather large author, Kevin Cummings recently. Kevin has some interesting insights into the world of literature, fashion, shoes, and the City of Angels.

Joe: How long have you lived in Bangkok, and where else have you found yourself, over the years? Also, what do you enjoy about living here?

KC: On average I have lived in Bangkok for 75% of each year since 2001. Over the course of my lifetime I have circumnavigated Balboa Island in a dinghy, panned for gold in the creeks of Auburn, California, played hoops for Chico State, and worked on Market Street in San Francisco. What I enjoy most about Bangkok is the anonymity, but now that that's over I still enjoy the street food.

Joe: How did you hear about Charlie's Design Fashion House?

KC: Late last year I was listening to Billy Gibbons when my Bangkok 101 Magazine arrived. Inside I read an article, "The Sharp Dressed Man". I then did some research on Bangkok tailors, and this was the clincher, I was impressed with your web-site design and your social media reviews, plus I've always liked the buzz on Sukhumvit 16, even though it's tucked away from the other even and odd sois.

Me and Joe

Joe: Your taste seems to have evolved since we first met you. What made you lose the Magnum P.I. look?

KC: Peer pressure, mostly. They convinced me the 80s were over.

Joe: You have written about some of the more interesting creative people living in and visiting Thailand in your debut book 'Bangkok Beat.' How did you decide what material to write about?

KC: I knew what I didn't want to write about: food, travel, conquests and Go Go bars. I wrote a book that I would find interesting, with the help of the best poet in Southeast Asia, John Gartland , ace storyteller and historical fiction thriller writer, Thom Locke, and pro photographers Eric Nelson and Alasdair McLeod. The book will have been out three years. It has aged pretty well.

Joe: What writers were your early influencers?

KC: Kurt Vonnegut, Ken Kesey, Philip Roth and Gary Trudeau. I like humor when it adds to the neurosis.

Joe: When did you first consider yourself a writer?

KC: I don't consider myself a writer. I like to write. The distinction is similar to a profession-al violinist and a country fiddler. Both pursuits are admirable and both are skill-sets. It's not easy for the fiddler to make a living fiddling, for one thing.

Joe: What do you like to wear when you write?

KC: My Bangkok Soi Dog #1 T-shirt with art by Chris Coles. I have several.

Joe: What's the one item of clothing that every man should have in his closet?

KC: A good quality bathrobe, un-monogrammed, long enough to meet the knee while sitting. Charlie Rose would still have a job if he had only donned one.

Joe: What will *Different Drummers* be about?

KC: My publisher, Frog in the Mirror Press, prodded me along with a few fans of the first book to write a sequel. John Gartland, Thom Locke, and Alasdair McLeod are once again on board. And I'll purchase some Eric Nelson photos at our standard rate. Without their contributions I wouldn't do it, simply because it wouldn't be as much fun or as good. The title and cover art are done. Bangkok Beat Redux is the sub-title. The Tokyo Joe's to Queen Bee story will be told, among others, and who wouldn't want to read about that? If you're reading this interview on paper that means all went according to Hoyle.

Joe: What writers living in Thailand do you admire?

KC: Robin Williams long ago said of the Hollywood crowd, "There's Jack (Nicholson), and then there is everybody else." At this moment in time there is Lawrence Osborne and then there is everybody else. I've heard Lawrence has a good sense of humor for an English gentleman. Anyone who likes Bill Murray is okay in my book.

Of the top tier writers, in addition to their writing abilities, I admire their doing. Joe Cummings, Jim Algie, Christopher G. Moore, Colin Cotterill, Jim Newport, Collin Piprell, John Fengler, John Burdett, to name a handful. They all live fully. They skip the hibernating season for the most part. They prepare for death far better than the average bear. That's what I find most admirable about good writers.

Joe: Finally, you've lived an interesting life, by some people's standards. What's next for you?

KC: A linen blazer. After that, as my wife likes to say, we'll have to wait and see.

Kevin is wearing a Chinese- sourced waffle-cloth bathrobe made by Charlie's Design, paired with Maui Jim sunglasses and a Bangkok Soi Dog #1 T. (All photographs by Alasdair McLeod)

CHAPTER 30

Read Any Good Bad Books Lately?

In 1945 none other than George Orwell wrote an essay titled, "Good Bad Books". What did George have to say about the subject at the time, and has the definition changed any in the last 70 years?

According to Orwell the term "good bad books" was coined by G. K. Chesterton, an English writer, poet, philosopher, journalist, and critic.

Orwell characterized good bad books as escape literature, and said their existence was due to "the fact that one can be amused or excited or even moved by a book that one's intellect simply refuses to take seriously." Among the books he includes in this category are the *Sherlock Holmes* novels by Arthur Conan Doyle, *We the Accused* by Ernest Raymond, *Dr Nikola* a Tibetan thriller by Guy Boothby, *Dracula* by Bram Stoker, *King Soloman's Mines by* Henry Rider Haggard, which has the honor of being made into a motion picture screenplay five different times. Orwell suggests that the supreme example of a "good bad book" is *Uncle Tom's Cabin* by Harriet Beecher Stowe: "It is an unintentionally ludicrous book, full of preposterous melodramatic incidents; it is also deeply moving and essentially true." Orwell never traveled to the USA during his lifetime but that never stopped him from opining on American literature or culture.

George Orwell concedes the need for the distraction light literature provides, and further acknowledges that "there is such a thing as sheer skill, or native grace, which may have more survival value than erudition or intellectual power." Orwell felt that most of the good bad books were written in the 19th Century and the early part of the 20th century but not at the time of his essay. As he wrote, "A type of book which we hardly seem to produce these days."

Like many people I enjoy a good bad book on occasion. Maybe too often, given the choices available. I think it is safe to say there has been an increase in such books since Orwell's day. Certainly there has been an increase in bad books, period. Reading a bad book is never a pleasant way to pass the time. When I think of my first good bad book it would have to be *Valley of the Dolls* by Jacqueline Susann. Some of the tougher critics might include Arthur Hailey's *Airport, Hotel,* and *The Money Changers.* I read all three and enjoyed them all. I read most of Vonnegut's work but found *Slapstick* disappointing. Hi ho. Was *Slapstick* a good bad book or just a bad Vonnegut book? I'm not sure. Vonnegut gave the novel a grade of "D" in his notable report card grades of his books. One of only two D's he handed out (Slaughterhouse Five got an A-).

My ultimate good bad book is, *The Lady in the Lake* by Raymond Chandler. It was Chandler's fourth novel, and my first and least favorite Chandler. It is well written but I figured out the mystery part in the first third of the book. That's never a good thing. Chandler is great at describing the outside of a building but less adept at detailing the inner workings of a character's mind (in that particular novel anyway). What about you? Have you read any good bad books lately?

CHAPTER 31

A Short Story for Papa – A Childhood Reminiscence

Wꜱhen I was ten years old we had just moved from Long Beach to Hayward, California. My grandfather who had been living in Oakland was suffering from emphysema and had moved in with us. He was a stubborn old cuss at times and as tight with the dollar as any man alive. I am convinced that is why his two sons were always so generous to me over the years.

My Grandfather, Papa I called him, got ready for his daily walk. My Mom said, "Go for a walk with your grandfather." So I did. We were living in a tree-shaded two-story house that had a creek run right through our back-yard, complete with a little arched bridge. But we headed out the front door and towards the bigger bridge that crossed a bigger creek.

Papa's breath was very labored and I could sense that, were it not for my presence, he wanted to stop to rest. I was sure he was trying to impress me. This confused the young boy that I was because my Grandfather was my hero. He was the best fisherman, carpenter, mechanic, handyman I have ever known. I was scared to death of him at times, but he was still my hero.

Papa introduced me to drop-line, pier, and deep sea fishing. Today I thought of him because it was my breath labored as if my lungs were covered in tar from decades of smoking Pall Mall cigarettes and working around asbestos in the shipyards of Berkeley as a ship-builder during World War II. Because I was walking up thirty flights of stairs for the first time in a long time. I won't tell you how long it took me, but I made it. And when I walked in the door of my Bangkok condo an hour before I wrote these words my wife looked at me with a big smile on her face and uttered those three little words every man approaching his 64th birthday needs to hear, "You're still alive!"

Damn straight. Thanks, Papa, for the memory and the tad of stubbornness that passed through the gene pool.

The End

Please proceed to the selected poetry of John Gartland.

CHAPTER 32
Witness Statements
The Poetry of John Gartland

Under Control by Ronald Merkesteijn

1

Stacked (with Mose Allison)

A painter once scoffed I had books at home,
so many disordered old books at home;
"It's nothing but a termite farm, your home,
I'd bin those books, keep 'em on my phone."

Love this one, love that one....
stack this one, stack that one.

I've just re-assembled my termite farm,
I've been years away from my termite farm.
So glad to be back on my termite farm
that's "never never done no man no harm",
loved this one, loved that one,
stack this one, stack that one.

Cleaned up my books and I pleased my wife.
Cleaned up my books and it pleased my wife.
Cleaned up my books and it pleased my wife
and I'm dustin' off footsteps of my life,
loved this one, love that one,
stack this one, stack that one.

And I'm sittin' over here at the six and nine,
just sittin' over here at the six and nine.
Just sittin' over here at the six and nine
got the best-read termites back in line,
love this one, loved that one....
stack this one, stack that one.

Spent days organisin' these termite stacks.
Long days organisin' these termite stacks.
Spent days organisin' these termite stacks
I got "time's winged chariot" at my back,
loved this one, love that one….
stack this one, stack that one…
Spent days organisin' my termite stacks,
Long days organisin' these termite stacks.
Spent days organisin' these termite stacks
and I found my peace and I'm back on track.
Loved this one, love that one….
stack this one, stack that one….
loved this one, love that one….

2

overheardinrehab

Systems Analysis ran my appraisal last week.
The silence following my result is ominous.
The scan exposed my social intercourse,
above the water line, as relatively, nothing.
And my career has reached its terminus.
The real Titanic-opener, of course,
(and this, H.R. found shocking)
the submerged mountain of my life
is mostly made of scoffing.
I am exposed, as no team-player.
The rich, the feudal and the sacred
invoke a scurrilous contempt which shows up
on my x-rays. My skeptical molecular conjunctions
are betrayed by science, and it's retrograde,
says H.R., career-wise, real bad luck,
to have it flagged, so obviously,
that you don't give a fuck.

But it is what it is, the consultant fluted.
Such heretical programming, so deeply rooted
will always be dangerous; and that's
how Ptolemy got his lobotomy,

they're telling me.

3

Rust-Belt Cantos # 3

Mapping many reasons
to commemorate these people,
the dispossessed, the left-behind,
the spurned detritus of the rust belt;
some, the hallmarks of humanity,
a vanishing , authentic kind;
the scarred, and the unfashionable stoics
of the steelworks and the coalface,
ironic as a breed, not given much to vanity.

As a boy he never understood that the
involuntary shaking of his father's hands was
still the nightmare aftershock of war.
That mother's iron discipline was forged in lonely
years before; a baby sister in her arms,
and crouched beneath the kitchen table,
wondering if she'd be able, ever,
to live through German bombing
of the factories along the river.

A testament of echoes, clues of parts:
bright fragments that I sift, and reassemble,
in this archaeological dig about the heart.

Remembering a time, of medical emergency;
when life in a polluted northern town
had brought pneumonia, lung collapse,
to me, a child of three, sent to a specialist
hospital far from home. Remembering
that sad cot, all alone, in a ward of colliers,
casualties of the local coalfields,

cuts me, still. Those doomed
and friendly giants, each day
trying to amuse me, calm my fears,
while wheezing to their early graves
from emphysema, silicosis, black lung.
Hard-cases Orwell wrote about;
the coal-dust crucifixions
on The Road to Wigan Pier.

4

Rust Belt Cantos #4

So, probe for clues, unpack the memory,
like an ark that's run aground here, and pursue
a testament of echoes, clues of parts;
bright fragments that I sift, and reassemble,
in this archaeological dig about the heart.

And somewhere, near the river, runs the line
of Thewlis Street, where Johnny Leigh, the draper
and pawn-broker, thrives upon a haunted corner.
And halfway up that terraced row, just there!
Jack Caslin's door. He looks up from his reading
in surprise; bespectacled and sitting in his chair;
smoke-stained clever fingers, thick, grey curly hair,
and welcomes us with laughter in his eyes.
Jack's house is full of sailing ships he's made,
so intricately rigged, becalmed in bottles,
so brightly painted, as a boy, I yearned to own them all.

Jack spent the war on convoys, bottled up in grey ships,
grateful for another day, without a lookout's call;
rolling with the dark and icy ocean. Fearful
that their hunted ships would never make a landfall;
coffined by steel bulkheads; dogged with threat;
heartbeat to the engines' pulse, and dreaming,
waiting, smoking; studying how to sweat.
No feet walk in those places now,
but half a dozen vanished streets,
and all the lives they sheltered
cry for witnesses somehow.
Smiling Esther, who'd been pretty in her time,
serves me a slice of Battenburg I toy with.

I'm more taken with the sideboard and its ships in bottles;
and, centerpiece, Jack's curious ocean clock.
A storm-tossed ship inside, rises and falls on a felt -green sea.

Behind pitching walls of ocean shines a far-off light,
on and off, regular as breathing, small as memory,
that guides me back to find Jack's masterpiece;
across the rolling years to sail,
and stand, a child, apart;
to where I watch Jack weeping,
on the day of Esther's funeral,
at the church of the Sacred Heart.

Bright fragments that I sift and reassemble.
Gold and wormwood, sunk beneath this place.
Words and faces,
strewn like broken driftwood on the dunes.
Consequences long obscured,
chances taken, births and partings,
hopes deferred and lives consumed;
recorded on the wind and rain
in this deconsecrated space.

A rush of unremembering accelerates around us.
This map, in ragged pieces, I have kept in any case.

5

Shot: Rust Belt Cantos: 5

Deakin has one lung,
the knowing smile possessed by medical enigmas,
and a catastrophic cough.
But while he's operating this infernal blaster
it's enough, to morph him to a god.
I remember that raised arm and warning nod
before he'd start the dread machine.
Recall him then resembling most
some fearsome, silt-encrusted Zeus
dredged-up from the Otranto Sill,
the mighty arm commanding, still,
and raised in ghostly power from antiquity.
Deakin's doomed and rust-stained figure,
wears iconic awe when trawled-up,
even now, from memory.

It's as if a thousand shot-guns fired continuously
scour the armoured heart of his machine,
and rusty steel and pit-props we must clean
are lowered from a roof crane,
creep, on moving entry rollers
through the rubber curtains, into hell.
The roar of it vibrates you to your bones,
will pulverise your very molecules,
as well as cleaning all the plates of rust,
which blows out as corrosive dust
into our badly vented factory.
And in bronchitic ritual, one more time,
gaunt Deakin rides the pristine steel emerging
on the exit rollers, wielding a compressed- air line,

and blowing off residual dust and taint,
before the sprayers, next, with oxide paint,
protect it, and enrich the caustic air.

That acrid murk will penetrate each hour
the flimsy masks we wear (and Deakin shuns).
As armoured flywheels hurl their numbing
violence within, inexorably his drama runs,
the chaos of a thousand guns, devouring him;
each shift, more hollowed-out with borrowed power.

6

Exemption clause

So, you made it
through the payroll years
and this phase came to pass,
a prostate like a frankfurter,
another bloody funeral,
and God's hand up your ass.
A vetriloquist's dummy,
a borrowed script
and a stranger for a wife,
a proctologist's glove puppet,
with a blockchain for a life.
Prosthetic imbecility now
power-assists the age,
malignant infestations breed
a biomass of rage.
But poet and philosopher,
perennially poor,
find there is consolation
being closer to the door.

7

from ... Director's Notes

"How many of these risky
foreign rooms have you unpacked in ?
Look, it's a walk-on in the prequel
to the remake of a sequel,
you're not in someone's moral maxim.
In your game, scary sub-plots
drag you in, and you must
sometimes take a headlong dive
into the dark and deep.

The last nightmarish act
already fades. Keep faith,
the mike is live,
the show proceeds......"

8

Pulp Writer

A pulp-writer of old Pompei
formulaic and fat and admired in his day
was busy at work in a grand chateau
when the mountain decided to give it a go,

and so from its creative anus
nature played its part
producing hot trash
in a grandiose fart,

immortalizing scribbling cinders
and casually elevating ashes to art.

(afterHorace)

9

Cantos of Cred....
(portrait of the artist as his cv)

Chemical works, steelyards, warehouses, building sites,
van jobs, production lines and agency-hand jobs,
lab jobs, limo jobs, telesales flying kites.
Band-jobs, night porter, farm-hand, labourer,
television-trainer, bin-man, cleaner, caretaker.
Professor, and barman, market trader, baker.
Shift-work on a shot- blaster, straight out of Dante,
hearse-driver, corpse collector, upping the ante.
Sales director, lifeguard, curator of a geode store,
repo-driver, teacher-in-five-countries,
sales promotion, door-to-door.
Copier salesman, not forgetting States-side, car-delivery driver,
voice and data-networks sales, and risky leasing-deal high-diver.
Freelance writer, interviewer, editor and studio-hand,
incognito pamphlet-writer, lyricist for a metal band.

Yes, done a few rough jobs ,
and that's a fact, loader, loaded,
packer, packed. Explosives branch,
factory inspectorate, signed
the-official-secrets-act.
Was a teacher in EFL zombie-world,
Asian lalaland deep cover,
been fucked over, moved on,
learned the ropes in tough schools;
made hay while the sun shone,
necessarily bent some rules.

Versatile, adaptable,
still learning new positions.
Juggling sin and syntax
till the final life transition.

10

Sightings

That's Fengler, if I'm not mistaken,
panama hat, and cigarillo;
goatee, from disguises 101.
He's flourishing a wine list,
and he's polishing an apercu.
Is he just pleased to see us,
or is he carrying a gun?
I'll be damned if that's not Fengler,
doing absinthe in the bar,
yes, I could swear it was Fengler
glad-handing bar girls or
photographing hors d'oeuvres,
and wasn't that Fengler
jumping on Mekong boats
and sharing his travel notes
while strumming a guitar?
I thought I saw Fengler, but
I could have been wrong,
at a juke-joint in Langley
spinning Johnny Cash songs.

Hey, wasn't that Fengler
with the chick and the cool,
mastering hit and myth,
and telling it old-school?
Yes, that was most likely Fengler.
Fengler, our louche raconteur,
checking into the Lux and
dispensing the lore.
Yes I think that was probably Fengler.
Yes, I think that was Fengler, for sure.

11

from ... Luck and Blood

My mother told how,
in the next World War, she
nursed a baby girl alone, with
dad away on active service.
His father came, demanding dad's blue suit,
"Because he won't be home to wear it".
She knocked his hat off,
beat him from the door
and never forgave him or forgot.
So, in a lot of ways
that shaped my views of him;
that and his unfriendly silences.
An analytical chemist, and
no easy man to analyse,
I saw him through my mother's
angry, father's disappointed eyes.

All, actors of chaotic past,
whose stories, now, I'm struck, I
walk the tightrope of their fates
to tell; must marvel at the luck
that gives a voice to this rich dust.

And behind him twists the mantra,
like a corpse upon a gibbet,
of the battles he had been through,
Ypres, Arras and the Somme....

12

Folded

Around us circle quiet shapes;
light glazing papery skin
and fragile hands,
dried flowers that flatter
the table of offerings.

Congratulate the maker
of these guttering lanterns.
Pour tea in cups of green lacquer.
Admire the understated
mastery of lives,
exquisitely folded
into the crumbling room.

13

from... Behind Bars # 1

A drunken queen crashes to the earth
mouthing endearments.
The bar girls laugh and hustle pool,
obsessives air their dramas, re-examine
what is real and what's illusory,
like actors worrying a part.

In Jack's place theatre is the rule;
shooting stars and spacedust,
bad actors from another galaxy,
the glass half-full, of smoke and blues;
continuing, imperfect art.

14

from ... History

From way-back in the records
it's been slavery-with-a-smile;
punishment and politicking,
mouthings of the priesthood,
from some poisonous old page.
Your life is a vicarious act;
a circus of surveillance
and a badly done soliloquy,
your inner script's a masterpiece;
remorseless, wounded rage.

15

And pity the mad shopkeepers

shackled to tedium
guarding the white goods
endless continuum,

a life-long walk-on
in theatres of trash,
in faustian transactions
of lifetimes, for cash,

feckless consumers and ambling drones,
couturier cretins enslaved by their phones.

And pity the mad shopkeepers,
shackled to tedium

guarding the white-goods
endless-continuum.

16

Poetics #1

Inspiration or disorder, I no longer care,
but from where I stand it's always
been clear that there's something
undeniably big, in the air.....

17

Framed

A broken sleep;
with strangers,
out of Sukhumvit as bars close.
On the night bus to Cambodia
your visa page is questioned
in a borderland of dreams.
The old address was overstayed,
relationships, all out of date;
the small print changed,
and far too late
you're suddenly afraid.

The Absurd, meanwhile,
in countless acts,
advances.
Still featured in the cast,
you re-enact flawed parts,
in dramas and romances.
Reprise your questioned role
within a love that did not last.
Act out the old illicit game,
discover recollection framed you,
then mis-spelled your name;

where you are hung, unvarnished,
with desire, and death, and blame.

18

from ... Real

The wreckage of knifers, pooling in cubicles,
gunshot and accident, pain and debris,
drowning drunks and mangled bikers,
irrational violence, drug OD's.
Those petrified faces spin off into silence.
Anonymous exit-smears, vomit on floors.
Morgue-fodder wheels out,
And more damage comes in through
those infernal swinging doors.

An invisible man, to medics, on shift,
I swabbed the floors of blood and shit,
till break arrived, and, coffee–bound,
I'd sprinted to the elevator....

Some worker,
massaging a garbage bag
into a shiny sausage,
of coal-black pvc,
staring off into the void,
and squeezing absently.
His image loitered with me later,
and his insane mirth,
his quip of, "Afterbirths",
his grin, as he squeezed out,
at the Incinerator.

I never did complete my shift,
but, some days feel like Casualty,
and death is an attentive waiter.

Says, every year brings closer,
my return, to the Incinerator.

19

Penhsketches #1

Arrival, Phnom Penh ;
sketches of a sprawling relocation,
and when production needs it most,
what happened to the inspiration?
Seething traffic moves by bat-squeaks
of horns, and some chaotic intuition;
magnetic fields, unseen, defy disaster,
purge and earthquake; an asteroid collision.
You're in a 3D re-make of the grand bizarre.
This is the first take.

Be careful, traveler;
this weirdness
might be who you are.

20

Penhdulum

The unfortunate kingdom
scarcely drew breath
between nightmares of yesterday
and the madness of king meth.
Street tarot readers search the times,
and hanged man is the ruling card.
Vain hope swings
to familiar paradigms;
benighted masses, streets of squalor,
terror, and an insane king.

21

Khmer Chasers

Bites on barbed wire.
Shots.
This is funky grotesque
from the cellars.
Ambience of blood-soaked
boulevards and slavish squalor,
uniquely aged in paranoia,
liquidised with dread
and Chinese bittters,
chilled in magisterial horror.
Instant showbiz. It's a
scary local act to follow.

In the Rouge Room
the old barman's back.
More shots.
Your head will hurt,
tomorrow.

22

Penhsketches #2

Under a flowering tamarind tree
a hot monsoon and darkness fell;
DZ, Phnom Penh, this cheap hotel.
Under a flowering tamarind tree
new landscapes are imprinting me,
re-learning escapology,
I lied to you, for you lied to me;
a fugitive heart, the lift of wheels
from airstrips of the slavish mind;
that grovelling acme of criminal deals,
that smiling madhouse, left behind.
I lied to you, for you lied to me.
And the future's sold to tyranny,
under a flowering tamarind tree.

23

Pepys in Penh #3

At a Riverside tavern
with the diarist, keep score
of pot-bellied gangsters
and predatory whores,
of old horrors immanent
and each folly consequent.

Since Maoists
killed the educated,
Penh counts the cost.

Here, imprinted nightmare
sustains the old order,
and daily life's lawless,
amnesiac dross.

Take coffee with tragedy
and smoke with a jest,
and as day unfolds its
unspeakable panoply;
elusive good fortune
decays with the rest.

24

Fortune Cookie

"Your terminal lucidity despises
the futility of human parts,
the flotsam of ideas, and
the vortex of defeated arts.
The aquifers are poisoned and
the oracle is paralyzed, they say.
And now that you have realized
all tragedy apes destiny,
conserve this spark good actor,
and take your lonely way.

(Colourful party-hat attached)."

25

from ....Noir shades

Now, wearing these, he's forced to see
political whoredom and organized theft,
hypocrisy, and insane greed,
the ignorant, feudal poor, bereft;
a walking nightmare he doesn't need.
Noir shades!

Sees rich men prostitute the law,
sees politics as puppet show, the
billionaires, temples, the rackets and gold,
sees an army of half a million slaves,
raped and bought and sold.
Noir shades!

Out on the street, a nightmare looms,
as fortune tellers cut the cards.
The truth is gagged. On the boulevards
all signs lead to the Rictus Rooms.
And behind the malls, the merit, and the smiles,
the clawing, desperate clutch of slaves.
Hard liquor cannot drive it from his head,
their smile, the victim-rictus of the dead.

Damn these infernal shades!
Once worn, he cannot take them from his head.
Once worn, he cannot take them from his head.

26

of tee-shirts

My alienation's on the sleeve
of an outsize Hamlet tee-shirt
badged "to see – or not to be".
I've stared too long into the void
and the void has outstared me.

(from thoughtsfromthewest)

27

from ..... The First Book of Inundations
Slippery God

On a bus on the Korat highway,
I had just received a call on the mobile
from my estranged wife (a novel enough event),
when we passed God on a motor cycle.
He was playing it safe and wearing a helmet,
but his black tee shirt was clearly marked, "God".
So I pondered if He was pulling the strings.
Divine intervention certainly
hadn't featured in our relationship before;
but maybe this was a new phase,
and, as a crush of clerics told me in my youth,
God works in mysterious ways;
and this seemed suitably ambiguous.
Moses got a burning bush that talked;
how would he have responded to the Godhead appearing
as just another Thai motor cyclist with his head up his ass?
Inadequacy is scarcely adequate to describe my feelings.
Why this call from my wife (estranged)
followed by Jahwe (retired) on a Honda?
A deluge commenced, intense even for the rainy season.
Cement factories glowed in the storm like…
like fiery arks. Was ark building an option?

28

Gilt

Serene psoriasis of the temple Buddha.
A face of peeling gilt,
plastered with the desperate
superstitions of the faithful,
buying incense and flowers;
bowing, kneeling, circling
and appealing
to invisible, ancestral powers.

A bribe buys everything
outside the temple walls.
So it's correct,
arranging such transactions
falls, within, to monks;
who, chanting, do the lucky deal,
and, poker-faced,
collect.

29

Snowline Sutra

Each bigot and fool is a learning tool,
each blithe hypocrite is instruction,
each liar and fake shows the moves not to make
in avoiding your moral destruction.
The highway to truth is a fabulous road,
often frozen and rocky and lost,
your noble objective, if not plain quixotic,
will come at a personal cost.
You will travel a way of precipitous peaks,
where runs only the natural law,
you will question all certainties, question yourself,
will know skirmishes, struggle, and awe.
The flock seeks the comforting rule of the shepherd,
and rats, the convivial burrow,
while they hide from the light
and consume their own shit,
you'll be scouting the snowline tomorrow.

And when, as it must, it will all come to naught,
a grail-quest, a saga of loss,
you'll be grateful life gave you the way of the wolf,
and these lonely, high passes to cross.

30

"It is important to note that there is no universal consensus on the definition of a fall. A recent Cochrane review reported that most studies fail to specify the operational definition of falls.... this leaves room for many different interpretations of a fall, and ......even a small change in definition may have significant consequences on the results of a study."
(Epidemiology of Falling)

FALLING 101

Go back to where the Falling starts,
in that indentured garden where we got a lifetime part
as God's rebellious outcasts, naked and ashamed.
The Father's feudal hand gives no exemptions,
be you newborn babe or simpleton, your birthright's to be blamed.

Pain wiped all details of my fall from memory.
But I'd stepped off a bridge into the inky void, apparently.
My girl, who came out looking for me, stepped right off it too.
She'd landed in an icy river. I'd hit a steel pipe halfway down,
and then the ground. Came round in pieces,
one week later, in the ICU.

Spool back five years, to undergraduate days,
the opening of that fractured narrative, and
the last convulsive quadrant of the Sixties.
In the West, an age of incoherent outrage
at the bloodbath of the Vietnam War.
Revisit student protests, our uncompromising
credo of the Marxist dialectic, lived full-bore.
Street clashes were the proving ground for flip
iconoclasm. In a fading age of deference
they tapped rebellious pent-up rage at

patronising power, at pretentious public
pantomimes of royalty, at years of
finger-wagging priests and brutal hypocrites,
and beatings I endured through all my schooldays.
Schools saw me, in so many ways, as careless of authority,
responding to life's pricks with undue levity.
So I became a satirist, inevitably, and penned
a weekly column at a redbrick university,
as an activist achieved a minor local notoriety;
but wince, now, at the chainsaw
Marxist rhetoric that owned me.

If we live long enough, we recognise the wind-shear
moments that undid us or that changed our course forever.
And call them what you will, Furies of ancient myth,
the Jungian Shadow, playing us like puppets,
bad karma's compound interest coming due,
they do not bow to Marxist dialectics,
and if they offer second chances, such are very few.

So I'd stepped off a life, into the empty future. Mea culpa.
Where fate bleeds into accident, I must leave up to you.
But after weeks of healing, to restrict my sense of awe at this,
my second lease of life, to merely feeling grateful, would not do.
Mea culpa, mea culpa, mea maxima culpa.
I'd cut loose from a foundered past, and I would re-create myself
    anew.

I've done a score of jobs, and more, since that plunge into darkness,
from production lines to lifeguard, from professorships to steelyard.
Changed countries like apartments,
but I never gave up writing, always cast a cold eye,
travelling,

on lives that fell behind me like escapements of a dream.
Ran into Smith, years later, in North London. Smith was a campus
   leftist
way back when; more skilled at downing pints than making points,
   but then
was still a Marxist, and working as a journalist for some left-wing
   teachers' mag.
On learning of my latest incarnation, as a salesman, he'd scoffed
   loudly
in the bar at, "How the mighty are fallen". I remember his ironic cry
and that year clearly; I was writing my first novel, at the time, and
   that
the project had possessed me was a fact I felt no need to justify.

Some years after that, by Admiralty Arch, I hurried to a London
   meeting,
and in the throng, a ragged homeless man broke surface briefly,
and for a fleeting moment caught my eye; a look of owlish irony
I surely recognised. I looked back, Smith had vanished, beyond
   calling.
Turned silent persona in the tragedy of falling......

31

Horatio Grows Old

This is getting more alone,
when ghosts, more real than people
come to gather at your home.
Habituation to the nag
of old scars,
breaks received and given.
This is getting more alone.
And all of those remembered faces
driven back on anecdote by scrum of years,
to stubbornness and stoic humour,
creeping fear's old antidote;
you recognised a future
in their jawline and survivor's eyes.
You're getting like them;
why disguise the fact,
you are no paragon or tragic hero.
Denoument or mere anti-climax
beckons in your final act.
The fantasy of triumph fades.

Drink your breakfast tea with Camus;
and at dinner, Dionysian wine
with Nietzsche sets the tone;
heroic solitude and shades;
you started out, grow daily more,
essentially alone.
Lyric holds the elegiac future
in a dark embrace,
a tight affair, acknowledged by the wise.

Affirmatively, here's alone;
laugh, paint your giant laughter;
you escape in dancing smoke.

The rest is lies.

32

Journophobia

And breaking news, this hour highlights
hermetic hype, pre-fabricated scoops,
submissive corporate-bondage trips,
and narcissistic media-whores
performing biased loop-the-loops
as slavish journalistic teams on station
present full dictatorial penetration.

Then, conjuring new abominations,
this slippery PR news massage,
from teflon- slick politicos, and clerics,
should hypnotize a watching nation,
stir up fear and public outrage,
foster pro-regime hysterics,
keep opinions in their cage.

Watch macho anchors interview
the misinformed and fatuous, in close-up,
precede a sexy weather wrap,
with glam, show-business airheads,
back to back, whose auto-cued sincerities
endorse the network's
gang-rape of the verities.

Fade-to-black.

33

Mama Noi checks out of the Mambo Hotel

You will never know who she was, at the end.
Great courtesans are their own kind of royalty.
Captivating beauty, took so many prisoners,
wrote so many stories, amatory puzzles,
friendships, in a trade not known for loyalty.

Through years, a swirl of power-grabs and wars,
magnetic Noi drew galleries of the famous,
bewitched a host of ones we need not name;
her affairs, discreet revolving doors;
embraces and liaisons, storied and profane.
Oh yes, she had a captivating beauty,
and she made a final prisoner of fame.

Now she's gone I'm haunted by the lost times.
Being with her, in those days, was
like a breeze through wind chimes.
She didn't need red carpet, friend,
to effortlessly raise the game.

See, great courtesans are their own kind of royalty.

(the eye # 6)

34

Mekong Delta Blues

Penh to paper;
the scenario ….disjointed city. There,
unblinking flow of joy and squalor,
Mekong river sashays by.
Street Nine, Khmer market women
try on bright plumage, flutter where
the muso guy admires them, jokes, and haunts
his grubby market for another day of
penury and smokes; a black-clad exile
practising and story-telling, getting old,
obsessively recording, on a shoe-string,
one brief, immortal age along the river.
River of wonder, river of tears and rage.
Frayed conjuror's thumb-nail, I've seen
re-attached with superglue, picking out
defiant constellations we grew under;
eloquent flo-chart running through
the plot and turning pages of our days;
river of wonder, river of tears and rage.

Minko gets the mighty Mekong captured, to the letter.
From "Ma Vlast" to the Mekong Delta,
no one, since Janacek, did it better.

Disjointed city. On Street Nine,
Khmer market women flutter by,
try on bright plumage, fly;
like Mekong Delta time.

35

Notable Deaths

"They're writing new obituaries
for the dinosaurs, in Chicxulub,
extracting funeral rock-cores
from a crater floor in Yucatan.
Expect a fossil theme park
in the peak-ring, before long,
and, Stairway to Extinction
is the hit-song corporate planners
will adopt to launch the brand.

And, leading on-line obits is
the passing of the drummer,
out of Megadeath, the band.
He made his final exit on the stage.
A good location for a rocker to eject,
and one suspects he'd have preferred
that final page, to shufflng off
the mortal coil in bed.

No talk, among these tributary obits,
though, of more celebrity dead,
like truth, locked up in a madhouse,
strangled by political correctness,
or freedom, hacked to a religious death
by mullahs, in the public square.
Descriptions of their
wake outrun your tears.

Fanatic rides to madness.
A boy's-own yarn of suicidal Mafekin'
on ketamine, might take you there.

A barbarous century's
Kiplingesque repayments:
served up, blood-stained,
in arrears.

Truth and freedom now
have joined the great extinctions,
it appears."

36

The Gallery Guide: Klashorst

Theory, with Klashorst.
They left the creative tap running,
when they made Klashorst, folks.
He's an ever-cruising art shark.
Stops painting and fucking, and he dies.
A gusher, an atheist comedian,
and a grasp of western art's advised,
if you want to catch his best jokes.

Hallucinogenic demon breed.
Surrealist of junk, subverting
masters, satirizing Eros,
copiously spilling seed.
And, "They're lovin' it," pal,
so if you're wise, you'll
lock up any virgins that you prize.

Klashorst unbound.

What else shall we call him?
I have a hundred names,
incorrigible paint-slinger,
whorehouse outlaw,
Frans Hals, shoots up Jesse James,
quick- to-draw, and play the fool.

Erotic true north,
mesmeric Caligari
of the high Dutch School;
an era's madhouse doctor, the
unbound priapic apostate of cool.

Praxis with fries.
The artist must be serial heretic,
as we are made of onion skins
of lies and ideology,
an abiding muscularity of lust.
And so, the artist must be
our anarchic tour guide
on this free ride
from erotic zone to dust.

37

The Bubble

What whorish kind of gig is that?
Decreed to surrender to
an irresistible future of bright
illiterates, to sashay stylish to a
new dark age in decades. Your
graduates, who know decline
as a label on cute underwear,
never heard of Custer or Horatio
brother; they don't care or know
if this is a last stand. It's fries
and A.I. to go. It's an era
of robotic sex franchised by
government,
with everything in hand.
Control in a magnetic bubble.

Hell, no. Win or lose,
real poetry's going to get you out,
real poetry's going to get you into trouble.

(from penhsketches)

38

Production Notes: Fall of the Khmer Republic.

Cut to the murderous traitors of the moment,
parading in white uniforms by Phnom Penh's Palace walls,
sick of a murderous playboy king and his Louis Sixteenth fantasies;
zoom, as a new flag rises on the corrupt Khmer Republic,
intercut, with pogrom and more xenophobic butchery;
overdub, a unique pall, of utter darkness falls.

Offstage the would-be film-star king, bankrolled
by Chinese Opera, plays dynastic puppet,
compliantly herds his bovine subjects,
with time-honoured Buddhist feudal tales;
as Pol Pot, despatched, like a plague-rat, from China,
descends through the hell of the Ho Chi Minh Trail.

His crazy wife spurs his habitual insomnia,
screams atavistic hatred of Vietnamese allies.
Most secretive Chinese Opera players,
they head towards the play's dark centre,
as yet, the unidentified main actors,
in this malignant masterpiece of lies.

Khmer Rouge recruiting sergeants rain
incendiary madness from the West.
B52's that pulverize the forest and its people
have a legion of dumb corpses show
American lies, duplicitous and dirty as the rest.

The Republic lives five short and twisted years.
Now pan to the Yanks deserting more proxies,
and blundering from new tragedies of blood.
Credits, on their farewell, diplomatic, Judas kiss.

To black, with the Maoists' great leap forward,
into the foul Cambodian abyss.

39

Rambler

Covert cops spy on tourist groups and walkers.
Flags and pennants flutter in the monumental squares.
Armed troops loiter, eyeing animated talkers.
There's still some conversation and unfettered truth
in coffee shops,
at least, for now, for anyone who dares.

(penhsketches)

40

At the Red Fox

Sepia walls and melodrama,
ice-cold beers and marijuana.
In this place, storytellers come to die.
In a tavern out of Webster
re-upholstered for Cambodia, hear the
swirl of smoke, the darkest joke,
the raconteur of legend and
the dreamer's entertaining lie.

(Penh Street 136)

41

Getting it Wrong

A smudged autumn night.
One of our rare sessions in the bar.
Kin Lok, heaping up a single skin with dark tobacco,
had been talking about women, as he would when he relaxed;
and Singapore.
"How a simple smile can sometimes be misleading;
generate all kinds of problems for a man."
He rolled the neat white tube, and licked it.
Anticipating him somewhat, I said,
"Misreading someone's signals can."
"Something along those lines", he murmured;
tamped the dangling strands at each end with a ballpoint,
lit the roll-up, and began.

"Chinese. And she had warm, disarming ways.
In Singapore, a nightclub bar, she recognized me;
came across to say hello. We fell to talking.
Laughed and joked a while, about old friends, old times.
She'd grown up, since those far off days.
And, taken with her smile (you know how these things are)

I was reflecting, as she went back to her table,
that I'd never slept with her, and that my chance
was most unlikely to arise, to coin a phrase.

The meeting was forgotten,
once the parting words were said.
Or so I thought, mistakenly,
till later, as I turned to leave the washroom,
and this gun was at my head.

The strangled Afrikaner voice accused me
of designs upon his woman, of insulting him.

He asked me how I felt, there,
on the brink of being dead.

'You've got this wrong, so very wrong', I said.
My tongue stuck to my mouth.
The universe contracted to the smells
of gun oil, cloying aftershave, and fear;
to whisky on his breath.
The words I needed fled.
'What do you see?'
He jabbed the barrel in my face.
'What do you see?' he asked.
And it was near, 'I think I see my death', I said.
I couldn't say how long he made me sweat,
until he pushed me out into the club again.
I had to take the microphone, apologise
onstage for my presumption, his embarrassment.

I said what was required, until he nodded satisfaction,
swaggered back into his drinking and dismissed
this insignificant distraction from his life."

Kin's eyes assumed that glitter.
Some ironic, jet black stone.

"I phoned my younger brother. Said I'd had a little trouble,
but I'd need to stay around there, for appearances.
My face was too well known.
The Afrikaner drank till late. And when they left,
I thought that I'd hang out a little longer.

Just as well, since someone jumped him in the car park
with a Remington pump action. Cut him off below the knees.
He'd made a lot of enemies. Who did it? Hard to say.

But they didn't take his money, or his passport.
Perhaps her screaming, in the end, drove them away."

42

Travels with Cortes

The poor ate dirt and venerated buffalo,
sent daughters to lascivious aquaria.
Enslaved by priests,
they dreamed of motor cycles, Sat. TV,
were raised to kiss their chains, and feel superior.
The golden pyramid glowered over every public space,
to have its shadow fall on you was death,
to look upon it, speak its name, was death.
To mock the monkey chancellor
was dicing with your sanity;
we sold them Rolex, submarines,
exploited their psychotic vanity.

43

Gamers

In the premier league in the Hundred Years War,
Machiavelli was striker, and, reading his lore,
I defended the faith and exploited the poor.
When I was a king in the Hundred Years War,
I'd bow to a queen but I'd rise to a whore.
You'd choke on my logic and gnaw at my core
when I was a king in the Hundred Years War.

Now the network is full of explicit instructions
for insane exo-skeletal mental constructions.
Strap-on Duty or Politics, Religious addiction,
wear Mohammed or Hitler, with power and conviction.
Try a weekend as Nietzsche, let the Muse be your whore,
you can mainline De Sade in a blood-soaked tanktop,
when you are a king in the Hundred Years War.

Do everything king-size, man,
the network is full of explicit instructions
for insane exo-skeletal mental constructions.....

44

Plaque

At the bridge, in Castlebar, by Linenhall Street,
upon the old grey stone, I read a plaque,
"1798, (the now-forgotten) Captain Chambers,
of Longford Militia, held this bridge
against repeated Franco-Irish attack."
The shallow stream boasts car tyres, beer cans, sad debris.
Across the narrow street, now, a phone-fixer shop,
a charity shop, and a window-full of kitsch;
and long-forgotten Captain Chambers, who can clearly see
Humbert, the Che Guevara of Napoleon's First Republic,
and the pike-men of the Irish Rising,
surging forward, lethally surprising, from the west,
the stalwart Captain Chambers, is pronouncing life a bitch;
long-forgotten Captain Chambers,
his defenders sorely pressed, remarks,
the unpredictable bayonet-rush of history's
a bitch.

A sports store flanks him now,
and by degrees, inching up Main Street,
the shiny creep of German autos,
their drivers texting furiously,
perhaps for reinforcements,
as musketeers and pike-men, rank on rank
contest the bridge in bloody desperation,
advancing by the fabric store,
into the grape-shot desolation,
determined to prevail or die.

Main Street is corpses, cannon-smoke, and screams,
bright murder scythes through either bank
in battle, pitched for this polluted stream.

Minor player Captain Chambers
re-enacts his gory sub-plot
here, on this very haunted spot,
the slaughterhouse of pavement, where I stand.

So Chambers, our sad captain,
holds the bloody line and smokes,
and on the bitter irony of history's
bad jokes, reflects.

Reflects, and grimly nods,
his doomed and soldierly respects.

45

Sir Richard Burton (unplugged)

He wrote later of a tendency
to shamble, in the Kasbah,
when leaving his researches
in the club he shall not name.
It had been coming on for forty
years, and getting worse now,
and added handicap to every game.

At the foot of the crooked pyramid,
the mamasan painted her eyes with kohl,
her face was a mask of Horus,
dramatis personae all fed on his soul,
and nemesis haunted the acts he did
in his walk-on part in the chorus.

Club hubris served narcotic harlots
iced beers and phenomenal weed,
and hot event-planning, and group activities,
and anything else a scholar needs.
Its influence had greatly extended the corpus,
of erotic researches so much to his credit,
though note-taking frequently was tortuous,
and focus sometimes failed him in the edit.
Oh, and his wife burned all the notebooks, at his exit.

46

Life-enhancing things

to toast round a burning mosque.

An end to the clitoral mutilation of babies,
and the sexual grooming of minors,
an end to organised female slavery
and the murder of atheists,
an end to religious torture,
and homophobic barbarities.
Here's a funeral toast for their decapitated,
their incinerated, their crucified, their enforced amputees,
their acid-scarred victims of honour crimes,
and all their butchered innocents, worldwide.
Here's a toast to the revival of free thought,
to the triumph of the rational;

and toasted bacon sandwiches, of course,
that's only natural.

47

Chores

You cannot conceive of the yearning felt by ghosts
in that forcible retirement home of spooks,
for the simple folding of clean laundry,
vacuum-cleaning an apartment,
the scrubbing of a bathroom
or the dusting of old books.
Enjoy your chores.

Impatience is the squandering of riches,
this random play of light on landscape,
the benison of birdsong,
the reflections of a conscious mind.
Your shutter-click of knowing
animates an arid universe.
It is your thinking manufactures time.
Enjoy your chores.

48

Bangkok Air

It had to be the emanon bar,
I can't tell you how unhinged he was to see me.
We'd had a few of their specials and we were getting loose.
I'd probably be teetotal if it wasn't for this bar.
You get drunk of course, but, it goes without saying
(you're obviously a cultured man) that context is everything,
always, and juice is only juice.
He ordered a trio of witch killers, bottled in Japan,
it's thirty five percent; strontium and alcohol.
Bottle's so cold you can't put it down but
after a few pulls you aren't afraid of frost bite
or polar bears or even the Koran.
A couple of rats were foraging
confidently under a food stall opposite,
the cat, as usual, was in hiding.
The mamasan, as only she can
displayed her astounding assets to man
leaned across the bar and lit a smoke.

There's poison in the city air,
wherever you're residing.

It's the frisson before story time.
He looked his age, whatever it was,
but obviously he could tell a joke.
A surprising number of city folk
are masked for pollution apocalypse.
I haven't fully sussed it yet, but
it's like a horror movie set, and
maybe we don't know we've had our chips.

He allowed himself a long consoling toke.
Decomposition, baby, your place, or mine?
I hadn't planned on retirement
in a zombie social paradigm.

He looked his age, whatever it was,
but obviously he could tell a joke.

Took up where he'd begun
when an arch and sexy female voice says
are you sitting comfortably children?
Here's the latest shit from the oracle,
as she leaned across the bar and lit one;
do bars get better than this he asked
and I took that as frankly rhetorical.

She will eat you alive
but I will risk it he said,
then I'll describe it later.
I'm old, he laughed, and bent
by all the vortices of vice,
but I retain a certain skill
in my role as the narrator.

It's been poisonous for years out there
and will get worse tomorrow.
My advice to those outside this bar
is don't inhale, or swallow.

John Gartland on Sukhumvit Road
(Photograph by Eric Nelson)

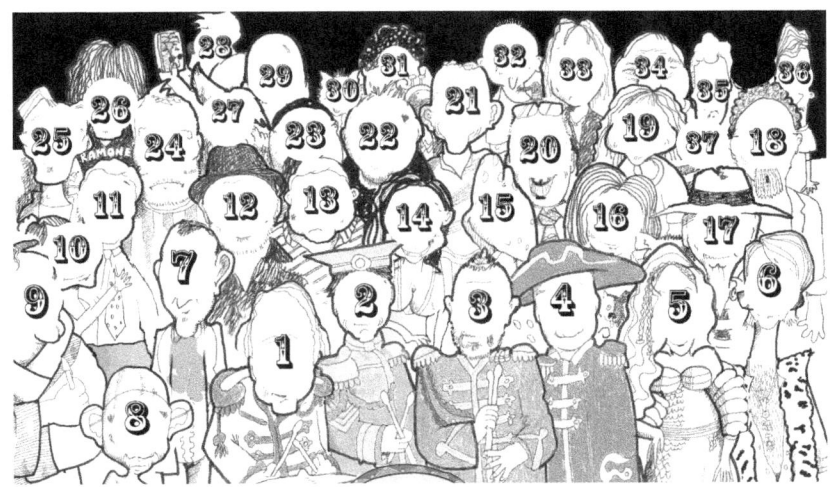

1. Kevin Cummings
2. Christopher G Moore
3. Colin Cotterill
4. John Burdett
5. Deni Hines
6. Von Von Von
7. John Gartland
8. Peter Klashorst
9. Lawrence Osborne
10. Jum Branton
11. John Branton
12. Kevin Wood
13. John Fengler
14. Mama Noi
15. Gop the Frog
16. Nichipa Armstrong
17. David Armstrong
18. Timothy Hallinan

19. Cara Black
20. Doug Stanhope
21. Chris Catto-Smith
22. Keith Nolan
23. Steven Segal
24. Collin Piprell
25. Jim Algie
26. Marky Ramone
27. Cotterill's Flipping Dog
28. Eric Nelson
29. Alasdair McLeod
30. Shilo the Chihuahua
31. Peter Montalbano
32. William Wait
33. Joe Cummings
34. Thom H Locke
35-36. Beavis and Butthead
37. Meghan Locke

Acknowledgements

In addition to all those who graced the cover of *Different Drummers* and those included between the sheets, kindest thanks are expressed to the photographers and artists whose work is too often underappreciated, swiped or unattributed (guilty). Specifically: Ronald Merkesteijn, Peter Klashorst, Eric Nelson, Alasdair McLeod, Steve Porte, Ken Sieczkowski, and Staton Winter.

Kindest Thanks

A special shout out to Colin Cotterill for his brilliant take on a simple idea. A book cover that would celebrate the iconic album cover of the Beatles Sgt. Pepper's Lonely Hearts Club Band on its 50th Anniversary. It is an album which solidified my appreciation for good music for a lifetime. Colin is also the illustrator for the Frog in the Mirror Press logo and occasional odd cartoons.

And for three of my favorite people in all of Bangkok, Chris Catto-Smith, Keith Nolan and John Branton, for keeping the music alive. To steal a line from our man On the Road to …, "Thanks for the memories."

Author's Note

Christopher Hitchens famously said, *"Everyone has a book inside them, which is exactly where I think it should, in most cases, remain"*. I miss Hitch. He was a wise man. His body is gone but his body-of-work remains. From the time I published *Bangkok Beat* in June of 2015, with the help of John Gartland and T. Hunt Locke, until now, with the publication of *Different Drummers*, many legends and loved ones of mine have died. Mark Fenn, of course, who led off this book, was one, also my older sister, Roxanne, and my high school basketball coach, Tom Barry, for whom *Bangkok Beat* was dedicated. Others are gone, Mama Noi – the longtime employee of Checkinn99, and Jerry Hopkins, author of, *No One Here Gets Out Alive*, among many. As Jerry knew, there will come a time when I, along with John, and Thom and the wonderful characters revealed in the pictures and pages in this book, will join them. Yet the Mama Noi stories will live on, and the poetry of John Gartland will live on, and *Bangkok Beat* and *Different Drummers* will live on, hopefully, in little pockets of a world we wouldn't recognize. Surely curio shops will still exist in the future? I'd love for a copy or two to end up there. The different drummers who grace the cover and pages of this book are a unique sample of those who have followed a different, less beaten path, in Southeast Asia.

I got lucky, and, while I acknowledge the necessary limitations, in compiling two ambitious and compendious books, I know I am better for having taken the journey. Thanks to you, all, for sharing it.

I will leave you by returning to a quote from another notable expatriate, and famous American author. He assisted me greatly without ever knowing,

"Develop an interest in life as you see it; the people, things, literature, music – the world is so rich, simply throbbing with rich treasures, beautiful souls and interesting people. Forget yourself."
—**Henry Miller**

About the Authors

Kevin Cummings

Kevin Cummings, born in Berkeley, California graduated from Placer High School in Auburn, California and California State University at Chico, where he played for the University basketball team. Since graduating he has worked in San Francisco, San Jose, Sacramento, Santa Cruz, California and Bangkok, Thailand. In 1999 he founded an Internet business supporting law offices and government agencies throughout the United States. In 2001 he met his future wife, Ratree, in Perth, Western Australia. Kevin divides his time between Thailand and California. He has been dubbed "the chronicler of the noir night". Kevin's blog, *Thailand Footprint*, may be followed at peoplethingsliterature.com. *Different Drummers* is his second book.

John Gartland

John Gartland, who is also an Irish citizen, was born in the industrial North West of England. He has travelled widely, and taught in five countries. He has been a steel worker, sales director, university lecturer, playwright, novelist and poet, and has a Master's Degree in Elizabethan and Shakespearian Drama. He excels in live readings of his poetry. Married, and resident in Bangkok, his published works can be found at, amazon.com/author/amazonjohngartland. Lizardville Productions features his poetry on Facebook @lizardvilleproductions.

T Hunt Locke

T Hunt Locke contributed the Mama Noi story set in 1960 and the Jim Algie interview to *Different Drummers*. Thomas is the owner and director of N.U. Test Prep Center in Northern Thailand. He is a loving husband and active father to his two growing children. Thomas is an accomplished writer of three different series of fiction. His most recent novel is, *Repent: A Bangkok Murder Mystery*. T Hunt Locke's books may be found at Amazon.com. You can follow his blog at thomlockepublishing.wordpress.com.

For More Information about *Different Drummers* go to:
PeopleThingsLiterature.com and

Bangkok Beat Store at: Bangkokbeat.bigcartel.com/products

Word-of-mouth advertising is needed by most authors. If you enjoyed
Different Drummers, please consider leaving a review on Amazon.
A few lines and a few minutes of your time will be appreciated.

www.ingramcontent.com/pod-product-compliance
Lightning Source LLC
Chambersburg PA
CBHW071243170626
46809CB00001B/79